*Otto von Frisch*

# MYNAHS

Everything about Purchase, Acclimation,
Nutrition, and Diseases

With Color Photos by Konrad Wothe and Other
Animal Photographers and
Drawings by Fritz W. Köhler

Translated from the German by Rita and Robert Kimber
Consulting Editor: Matthew M. Vriends, Ph.D.

**BARRON'S**

Woodbury, New York/London/Toronto/Sydney

First English language edition published in 1986 by Barron's Educational Series, Inc.

© 1981 by Gräfe und Unzer GmbH, München, West Germany

The title of the German book is *Der Beo*

*All inquiries should be addressed to:*
Barron's Educational Series, Inc.
113 Crossways Park Drive
Woodbury, New York 11797

International Standard Book No. 0-8120-3688-3

*Library of Congress Catalog Card No.* 86-10817

**Library of Congress Cataloging-in-Publication Data**

Frisch, Otto von.
  Mynahs : everything about purchase, acclimation, nutrition, and diseases.

  Translation of: Der Beo.
  Includes index.
  1. Mynahs. I. Title.
SF473.M9F7513 1986      636.6′869      86-10817
ISBN 0-8120-3688-3

Printed in Hong Kong

6 7 8 9          490          9 8 7 6 5 4 3 2 1

*Inside front cover:* Professor Otto von Frisch with his pet mynah Peter (photo by Rüppell).

Photographs: Coleman/Coates: Page 64 (above right and below, left); Coleman/Williams: Page 64 (below right); NHPA/Rao: Pages 46 (below) 64 (above left); Reinhard: Page 10 (above); Rüppell: Inside front cover; Wothe: Front cover, back cover, inside back cover, pages 9, 10 (below), 27, 28, 45, 46 (above), 63

*Professor Dr. Otto von Frisch*, son of the Nobel prize winner Dr. Karl von Frisch ("Frisch on Bees"), grew up surrounded by every conceivable kind of animal. His tame jackdaw "Tobby" and other birds were his childhood companions.

Otto von Frisch studied biology at Munich University with one year in the U.S.A. His doctorate, written in 1956, was on "The Breeding Biology and Early Development of the Curlew." Today he is director of the Natural History Museum in Braunchweig and professor at the Technical University of Braunschweig. In 1973 he received the German Children's Book Prize for his "1,000 Tricks with Camouflage."

# Contents

# Contents

# Preface

As a student I spent a year in the United States, where I was invited one evening to the house of a professor whose specialty was ornithology. I arrived rather late, and after the professor had introduced me to his wife and three children, we sat down to dinner. There was plenty to talk about, and I assumed the whole family was gathered around the table, but every so often I thought I heard somebody say something in the next room. At first I didn't pay too much attention, but finally I began to wonder. There seemed to be several persons in that room, or at least I heard several different voices. Then I distinctly heard a female voice say, "Good morning Mr. Emlen!" It was late in the evening, and I was totally puzzled. Mr. Emlen, my host, must have noticed the expression on my face. He looked up briefly and said, "Oh, that's just our mynah; he always talks a lot before going to sleep." Now my curiosity would not let me sit still any longer. I had, of course, heard of mynah birds and their talent for speaking, which is supposed to equal, if not surpass, that of parrots. But I had never seen one of these birds. So we went to the next room, and there, in a large cage, sat a magnificent mynah. Now that he had company, and perhaps animated by seeing a new face, he became truly loquacious. All I can remember at this point of the many words and sentences he produced was, "I think a storm is coming tomorrow," spoken in a worried tone and an exact imitation of the professor's voice. This was followed by the greeting in the hostess' voice: "Good morning, darling; the coffee is ready."

This mynah bird had a huge repertoire of phrases and sentences, all of which he pronounced in the various pitches and intonations the members of the household used. When he finally got tired he hopped to the cage floor, picked up a corner of the newpaper, crawled under it, and started to bark. Then he fell silent and apparently went to sleep. This performance impressed me deeply, and I determined then and there that some day I would own one of these birds. However, my wish went unfulfilled for almost twenty years. I had to wait until I had a house and garden of my own large enough to accommodate various "beasts," and it also took a while to find a supplier who could guarantee that the bird I bought was a youngster. Let me emphasize right here at the beginning that obtaining a bird as a fledgling or "gaper," as fledgling mynahs are called, is crucial if you want it to become hand-tame and to learn to imitate well. There will be numerous mentions of my first mynah, which responded to the name of Peter and lived for twelve years. But first we want to explore where mynahs come from and how they live in their native lands.

Otto von Frisch

# Where Mynahs Come From

## Their Lands of Origin

The Lesser India Hill Mynah occurs naturally in Sri Lanka (Ceylon) and in southwestern India as far north as the 17th degree of latitude. The Java Hill Mynah is distributed over a considerably larger area. It is found in some parts of the East Indies and of the Himalayas, from Kumaun to southern China, including Hainan; in Indochina as far south as Malaya, Sumatra, Borneo, Java, the Andaman and Nicobar Islands, as well as the smaller islands in this region, such as Palawan, Bali, Sumbawa, Flores, Pantar, and the Lesser Sunda Islands. It has also been introduced and become established on Christmas Island in the Indian Ocean and on Oahu Island (Hawaii). The distribution of the Ceylon Mynah is, as the name suggests, restricted to the island of Ceylon.

## How Do Mynahs Get to Our Countries?

The mynahs we find in pet stores usually have a long and arduous journey behind them. They are almost all young birds (gapers) that were taken from the nest as fledglings by natives and fed cooked rice mixed with a little chopped meat. When the mynahs are strong enough, they are transported by car to Thailand, and from there to dealers in Bangkok. These dealers keep them until the plumage is fully developed. During this period the birds are given a special mynah diet imported from Japan and fortified with vitamins. From Bangkok they are flown directly to America or Europe by air freight.

The exporter in Thailand informs the importer in the U.S.A. or Europe by telephone or telegram of the airplane's exact arrival time. This is of special importance because these young, tame mynahs still depend on being fed and would otherwise have to go hungry too long.

The importer then passes the mynahs on to government (for example USDA) import facilities where the birds will be transferred to various isolation cages. During a 30-day quarantine period, birds in the United States will be cared for by veterinarians and other personnel of USDA's Animal and Plant Health Inspection Service (APHIS). Other countries have similar rules. During the quarantine, veterinarians will test the birds to make certain they are free of any communicable poultry disease. Infected birds will be refused entry; at the owner's option they will either be returned to the country of origin (at the owner's expense) or humanely destroyed.

This scenario may sound straightforward enough on paper, but for the birds the long trip is a nightmare. It is not hard to imagine the strains and hardships they have to endure: a succession of new faces, different cages, and changes in climate and diet. Add to this daylight and darkness at unaccustomed hours and treatment that is undoubtedly not always as considerate and caring as one might wish. It is no wonder, then, that many a mynah in a pet store looks more like a little heap of misery than a relative of our cheerful starling.

The Society for the Preservation of

# *Where Mynahs Come From*

Lesser India Hill Mynah (above), Greater India Hill Mynah (center), and Java Hill Mynah (below). The most obvious difference between the three races is in the size, but they also have different markings on the head.

Nature and Wildlife of Sri Lanka has announced that the export of mynahs from that country is now illegal because these birds constitute a protected species. In earlier days they were captured with bait or fine nets or taken from nests in this country, too.

## What Family and Genus Does the Mynah Belong to?

Mynah birds belong to the family of starlings (Sturnidae), which includes our common local starling (*Sturnus vulgaris*). Most birds of this family are small to medium in size, have a shortish tail, and walk with a slow or waddling gait when moving on the ground.

Within the family of Sturnidae there are twelve species of mynahs. Hill Mynas, to which the imported cage birds belong, always have more or less pronounced yellow wattles (also called lobes or lappets) on the head. The Ceylon Mynah (*Gracula ptilogenys*) is the only mynah that lacks these wattles. Hill Mynahs (*G. religiosa*) occur in eleven subspecies, or races, found from Sri Lanka to Hainan.

On Sri Lanka we find two species of mynahs: the Java Hill Mynah (*Gracula religiosa religiosa*) and the Ceylon Mynah (*G. ptilogenys*). The Java Hill Mynah is quite common and often lives near human settlements and even in cities, if they have tall trees and parks. The Ceylon Mynah, on the other hand, prefers thickly wooded hill country between 1,000 to 6,000 feet (300–2,000 m) above sea level. The Ceylon

7

# *Where Mynahs Come From*

Mynah is hard to tame and avoids human contact.

Both the Java Hill Mynah and the Ceylon Mynah nest in cavities about 20 to 30 feet (7–10 m) above ground. Eggs are laid in February or March as well as from June to August.

## Hill Mynah Subspecies

Most of the imported mynahs belong to one of three subspecies of *Gracula religiosa*. They are the Lesser India Hill Mynah (*G. religiosa indica*), the Greater India Hill Mynah (*G. religiosa intermedia*), and the Java Hill Mynah (*G. religiosa religiosa*). Actually, it is not altogether clear yet whether *G. religiosa intermedia* should be considered a separate race or subspecies. The three races differ primarily in size: The Lesser India Hill Mynah measures about 9 1/2 to 10 1/4 inches (24–26 cm); the Greater India Hill Mynah, 10 1/4 to 11 3/4 inches (26–27.5 cm); and the Java Hill Mynah, up to 15 inches (38 cm). The Greater India and the Java Hill Mynahs have stouter bills and thicker legs than their smaller cousin; their bills are a deeper orange red; and the yellow skin patches on the head and the ear wattles are more pronounced.

## Some Close Relatives of the Hill Mynah

**Pagoda Mynah** or **Brahminy Starling** (*Sturnus pagodarum*)
*Size*: 8 inches (20 cm). *Distribution*: Eastern Afghanistan, Nepal, India, and Sri Lanka.

*Aviculture*: To be kept in large indoor aviaries or in outdoor aviaries with live shrubs. Withstands winter cold after acclimation. Pairs should be by themselves; single birds can be added to a mixed community. This bird is known for its talent at imitations. *Diet*: Food for soft-bills, small pieces of fruit, berries, soaked raisins, insects, low-fat cottage cheese, lean meat. If given access to insects, fruit, and raw red meat cut into small pieces, the Pagoda Mynah will breed in starling nesting boxes.

**Chestnut-tailed Starling, Gray-headed Starling,** or **Malabar Mynah** (*Sturnus malabaricus*)
*Size*: 8 inches (20 cm). *Distribution*: India, Sri Lanka, and Afghanistan. *Aviculture*: To be kept in large cages or in aviaries. Does not get along with smaller birds. Can winter outdoors if it has access to a shelter. *Diet*: Food for soft-bills, lots of fruit and berries, and insects.

**Superb Starling** (*Lamprotornis superbus*)
*Size*: 8 inches (20 cm). *Distribution*: Northwestern and northeastern Africa. *Aviculture*: Densely planted aviaries. Withstands winter cold if protected from rain and drafts. Single birds can be included in a mixed community; pairs are better kept separately. Aggressive during the mating season. The clutch consists of three to four blue-green eggs covered with bright reddish-brown or blue spots. The eggs hatch after

The daily bath—a pleasure you should not deprive your mynah of.

# Where Mynahs Come From

14 to 15 days. The Superb Starling prefers to use roomy parakeet boxes or nests made by blackbirds, orioles, or grackles. Since Superb Starlings breed readily—if they are kept in aviaries by themselves—the young of the first brood should be taken from the parents when it appears that a second brood has been started. *Diet*: Food for soft-bills, small pieces of fruit, berries, and insects.

## Purple Glossy Starling
(*Lamprotornis purpureus*)
*Size*: 9 inches (23 cm). *Distribution*: Southwestern Africa. *Aviculture:* To be kept in large indoor aviaries. Needs lots of room. Aggressive toward smaller birds. *Diet*: Primarily small pieces of fruit, insects, and berries.

## Splendid Glossy Starling
(*Lamprotornis splendidus*)
*Size*: 10 inches (25 cm). *Distribution*: Western Africa. *Aviculture:* The male is completely blue-black with a gorgeous metallic sheen in green-blue hues. Its eyes are pale yellow and the feet and beak are black. Pairs are better kept separately. Aggressive during the mating and breeding season. *Diet*: Food for soft-bills, mynah pellets, small pieces of fruit, berries, green food, and insects.

## Long-tailed Glossy Starling
(*Lamprotornis caudatus*)
*Size*: 18 to 21 inches (45–53 cm); tail 10 to

Mynahs are accomplished flyers. They are also able to rotate their heads 180 degrees.

13 inches (25–32 cm). *Distribution*: Northeastern and western Africa, particularly in woody areas but also in open terrain. *Aviculture:* Often seen in pairs or in families of six to eight, these lively birds can be quite dangerous to other birds in mixed collections. The bird is steel-green with metallic green and blue sheens, particularly on its back and tail. Both back and tail have black transverse stripes. This bird has a black eye-stripe as well, and, like its related species, it has yellow eyes. Its beak and feet are black. *Diet:* Same as for the Splendid Glossy Starling.

## Green Glossy Starling
(*Lamprotornis chalybaeus*)
*Size*: 9 to 10 1/2 inches (22–26 cm); the hen is a little smaller. *Distribution*: Northeastern Africa. *Aviculture:* The bird is predominantly steel-green and bluish in color, with a dark blue stomach and dark metallic-green tail. Its eyes are golden yellow; its feet and beak are black. These birds tame rapidly with good care, and they seem to be shown to better advantage in aviaries than in cages. They also love to bathe. When given live insects, the Green Glossy will breed sooner or later. The three (rarely five) eggs are light greenish-blue in color with fine reddish-brown and dark blue markings. In captivity, these birds soon shed their timid nature and remain very active. *Diet:* It is advisable to supplement their diet with lean ground beef, rice, and fruit. For more diet details, see the diet suggestions for the Splendid Glossy Starling.

# Considerations Before You Buy

## Basic Questions

Whether or not you decide to get a mynah should depend largely on how you answer the following three questions.
• Will I be able to look after the bird properly, and do I have plenty of time to keep him company?
• Are my living quarters large enough to accommodate a cage or aviary of proper size?
• Am I sure that the mynah's penetrating voice won't bother me in the long run? And am I willing to put up with the unpleasant aspects of keeping a bird, such as having to clean up droppings and spattered food?

If you have answered these questions with a yes, then you can go ahead and find yourself a mynah.

## Mynahs are Social Creatures

Mynahs are by nature sociable. This is not true of all birds. There are some that—at least outside the mating season—take little interest in their fellows and prefer a solitary existence most of the time. Such unsociable members of the avian world don't suffer from loneliness if they are isolated in captivity. But for gregarious species (including not only mynahs but also parakeets and parrots), being alone most of the time—often in a small cage—represents a serious deprivation. These birds not only remain shy and fail to develop trust in their keeper, but they also pine. They *need* company and communication. This does

not mean that you have to spend all day talking to your mynah. He will be perfectly content if he knows you are around and catches sight of you now and then, perhaps even in a different room. He can also be left alone for short periods of time. But if you leave every morning for work and don't come back till evening, if you like to spend weekends away from home, and if you plan to have someone else look after the bird during vacations, then you had better forget about owning a mynah.

## Male or Female?

In most species of the starling family the two genders are indistinguishable, and sexing mynahs on the basis of appearance or behavior is practically impossible. In addition, aviculturists have had almost no success in mating mynahs in captivity. The question of whether to get a male or female is therefore of little practical importance.

## A Mynah Needs Space, Lots of Space . . .

Mynahs are not only sociable but also extremely lively and active. They like to hop, walk, and fly. This means that they need adequate space to move around in if they are to feel comfortable and not become obese. Obesity can cause premature death. A daily session of free flying is thus essential for your mynah's well-being.

But since free flying involves some risks for the bird (see page 29) and also creates a certain amount of dirt, your mynah is likely to spend much of his time confined to his quarters. These quarters should at least consist of a standard mynah cage. Such a cage is about the same size as one for a large parrot, but it does not need to be as tall. Instead, it should be longer and wider. Never put a mynah in a cage designed for canaries or other small birds. Even a mynah cage offers your bird no more than the bare minimum of space he needs to move around in. An aviary where the bird has a chance to fly is obviously much better. But since you need a proper place for a large cage and an aviary, you had better begin by having a look around your apartment with this problem in mind.

## . . . and Can Screech Very Loudly

We have already said that mynahs are sociable and active birds, but we haven't yet considered how noisy they are. Like most birds they rise with the sun, if not earlier, and don't go to sleep until it gets dark outside or until you turn out the lights. In the summer months this makes for a long day. Mynahs are especially vocal before retiring at night (see page 56). Your bird's well-intentioned good-night wishes may in time get on your nerves, and your enthusiasm for him may diminish when his early alertness intrudes on your morning slumber. In a large house it is easy to find a place where the mynah can carry on as early or late as he pleases without disturbing anyone's rest or sleep. But in a small

apartment the bird's penetrating calls can become a serious nuisance. Even if you're not bothered by the noise, your neighbors may feel differently. Apartments in modern buildings often have thin walls, and you can practically hear a pin drop in your neighbor's rooms. Having a noisy mynah can, under these circumstances, cause friction with neighbors or your landlord and may possibly lead to problems with the police. When you consider the basic questions on page 15, also give some thought to the world outside your own four walls.

## Soft-bills Make a Lot of Dirt

Birds can be classified into seed-eaters and soft-bills. The latter, among which the mynah is numbered, are birds that feed primarily on insects and/or fruit. Seed-eaters, as the name suggests, eat mostly seeds. Parakeets, parrots, the various kinds of finches, and many of the exotic small birds that are kept by bird fanciers are seed eaters. If you watch a canary or parakeet eat, you'll see him pecking the sunflower or millet seeds, eating only the edible part of the kernels, and letting the empty hulls fall to the ground. Whatever the digestive system is unable to absorb is passed in the form of small droppings with a consistency of thick paste. Soft-bills, on the other hand, especially those that eat fruit, are sloppy, not to say wasteful, eaters. This may be because, where they live in nature, fruit is almost always available in abundance. What does it matter whether a fig is consumed in its entirety or is left half

# Considerations Before You Buy

uneaten? There are always more on the tree. Fruit moves through the intestinal tract even faster than other kinds of food and has a very high water content. This is reflected in the mynah's droppings, which are generally very wet and messy. Add to this the bird's untidy eating habits, and you'll realize that there will be plenty to clean up. The cage and its immediate surroundings have to be scrubbed every day, and if the mynah flies free in the room, the entire room usually needs cleaning.

When you get to the third question on page 15, ask yourself not only whether you can tolerate the noise of the bird but also whether you are prepared to take on the quite substantial cleaning chores.

## Other Points to Consider

It is certainly not my intention to talk you out of wanting to own a mynah, but I do want to raise a few other points you should be aware of before you make your final decision. It is better to think first and perhaps decide a mynah is not the bird for you than to realize too late a mynah is incompatible with your life's circumstances and then be faced with the problem of how to get rid of the bird.

You should know that a mynah needs proper care when you go away on vacation (see page 36) unless you take him along. You should be aware, too, that mynahs can live 12, 15, sometimes up to 25 years and that you are therefore entering a long-term relationship with the bird. You should also know that mynahs often don't get along with smaller birds and cannot always be introduced into a community aviary (see page 36). And finally, you should make no assumptions about a mynah's gift for mimicry (see page 52). Not every bird masters this art. It is conceivable that your mynah will never learn to produce a single human word and will be content to babble in his own language as long as he lives. The same is true of parrots. But these less gifted birds can become just as affectionate and enjoyable companions as more spectacularly talented ones.

## Some Important Tips for Buying

Now that you know some basic facts about mynahs, you are ready to go out and buy one if you are still convinced that this is the bird you want. Most pet stores routinely carry mynahs. The price is usually around 150 dollars for young birds, 200 dollars for babies, and 250 dollars for talking birds.

Unfortunately, most of the birds for sale are kept in cages that are much too small for them. Consequently they look dirty and ragged because they have no chance to keep themselves clean.

### Is There a Way to Tell Age, Health, and Special Qualities of a Mynah?

First of all, I want to impress three facts on you:
• There is no guarantee that any given mynah will turn into a good talker.
• There is no guarantee that the bird you buy will be as young as he should ideally be.

# Considerations Before You Buy

- There is no guarantee that your bird will be in perfect health.

Let us turn to the first point. Only time will tell whether or not you purchased a bird with a talent for speech. Of course chances are better if the bird already has a vocabulary or words and sounds when you buy him. But this is rarely the case. Needless to say, a mynah that already knows how to talk fetches a higher price or is not for sale at all.

As for the second point: Mutual adjustment is of course easier if the mynah you bring home is still very young. You can tell whether a young mynah is under six months old if he cannot yet fly properly because the flight feathers on wings and tail have not reached their full length and if he still opens his bill in a wide begging gape. Birds like these are very young indeed, practically still nestlings. They are hardly ever found in regular pet stores because their care is too time-consuming. Mynahs that can already fly but are under six months old differ from older birds in lacking their elders' metallic gray or purple sheen. The iridescence doesn't appear until after the first molt. The plumage of juvenile birds is more ash gray to dull black. But after the first molt there is no telling whether a mynah is one year old or ten.

And finally, our third point: How can you tell a sick bird from a healthy one? Often it is immediately apparent if there's something wrong, but not always. A bird can look perfectly normal and yet have a disease that may prove fatal. However, you're not likely to bring home a doomed bird if you examine your candidate thoroughly before purchase. But as I've said, there are no guarantees.

I would urge you, if at all possible, to take along a knowledgeable bird fancier when you set out to buy your mynah. The information and advice given by salespersons is not always reliable. The majority of dealers are honest folk, but you may run into an unscrupulous individual intent on palming off a weak or sick bird before it dies. If your newly purchased mynah succumbs to illness a few days after you bring it home, complaints are usually fruitless and you have no further recourse.

## What to Watch Out for When You Buy a Bird

Be as shrewd and cautious when you buy a mynah as when you're in the market for a used car or about to invest in some valuable object. Pay special attention to:

- The plumage.

Does it form a clean, smooth, unbroken coat?

Or is it dirty and untidy with bare spots, especially on the head and neck?

- The legs.

Are they clean, and do the horny scales lie flat against the legs and toes?

Or are they chapped and dirty, with scales sticking out? Are some toes misshapen or missing altogether? Are the toenails too long and curled out of shape?

- General behavior.

Does the bird look lively and content? Is he hopping around, eating, drinking, and preening himself? Is he observing his surroundings with interest?

# Considerations Before You Buy

Or is he sitting in one spot all puffed up, with eyes closed, breathing with difficulty, and indifferent to the world around him?
- The droppings.

Are they passed from time to time without visible effort? Are the feathers around the vent clean? Are the droppings, though runny or mushy, of an even consistency?

Or is the mynah straining in vain, with rocking motions of the body, trying to produce droppings? Are the feathers around the vent filthy and sticky, or are there watery bubbles in the excreta?

If you observe even one of the negative signs listed, refrain from buying the bird. Point out to the dealer that that particular bird is sick and should not be offered for sale.

### Caution Against Buying Birds by Mail

If you have a chance to watch a mynah at your leisure before you buy it, you have a good idea of what you're getting. This is not the case if you buy from a big mail order company. You'll have to order from a list, and you have no say about what is sent to you. You won't know what you're getting until you open the package. If the bird is sick or injured, and even if it is dead, you are usually not entitled to a replacement. (Check on this before you order.)

If you should receive a sick or dead bird, have the post-office official or deliveryman give you a testimonial in writing of the bird's condition upon arrival. But I myself would not take a chance on ordering from a catalogue unless I knew that the firm had an exceptionally good reputation.

## A Word about the Protection of Wild Animal Species

Mynahs are not among those cage birds that reproduce readily in captivity. Every mynah you see in a pet store was taken from its natural habitat and will not return there. It is true that in some of the countries that export mynahs these birds are not listed among endangered species. They may therefore be legally sold, but by buying a mynah you are supporting the trade in wild animals. The decision is up to you whether you want to contribute to the reduction of wild bird populations. A major dealer in birds and other pets has told me that India ceased exporting both the Lesser and Greater India Hill Mynahs a number of years ago.

The reason for this is presumably that Indian mynah populations have been decimated too drastically. Now mynahs are imported from Thailand. Peasants there make a living almost exclusively from selling young mynahs (gapers) to dealers in Bangkok. The birds that arrive in Bangkok already have a journey of several hundred miles behind them, and they then embark on a flight to Europe or America. There are no figures about what percentage of the birds perish in transit.

# *What a Mynah Needs to Thrive*

## The Right Cage

A cage for a mynah has to be at least as large as one for a large parrot, such as the Gray or the Amazon Parrot. This means that the cage should measure at least 20 x 20 x 20 inches (50 x 50 x 100 cm; see drawing below). But even a cage of these proportions is quite inadequate if the bird spends all its time there because the cage does not offer enough room for the mynah to indulge its natural need for movement.

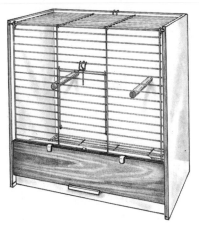

This drawing shows a good cage for a mynah. It does not have to be open on all sides, but the bottom should be removable (like a drawer) so that you can clean it easily.

As a consequence, the bird quickly gains excess weight. If you have no room for a larger cage, you'll have to let your mynah fly free in the room every day (see page 29). Cages designed for parrots generally are taller than they are wide and long.

Because parrots are climbers, this suits them well. By using their feet and beak they can easily move up and down the cage walls. Mynahs, however, are not climbers; instead, they like to hop. Hopping up and down on walls is a lot more difficult than hopping on even ground, and that is why a cage for a mynah should be wider and longer than it is tall. Unfortunately, cages of these dimensions are hardly ever offered for sale, and you'll either have to build one yourself or have it made to order. Since mynahs do not use their bills to chomp on wood or thin wire—a habit that forms one of life's main pleasures for parrots and parakeets—the cage you build need not be particularly sturdy. All that matters is that it be practical—for you as well as for the bird.

A mynah cage need not be open on all sides. If the front and one side wall consist of metal bars, the rest, including the roof, can be made of wood. In fact, most birds like the sense of protection that a solid roof and back give them. The solid walls also reduce or eliminate drafts.

The open parts of the cage can be constructed of metal bars or welded wire mesh, but the metal should be chrome plated so that it will withstand frequent washing. Nothing that rusts will do. It is also important that the spaces between the bars or in the mesh not be large enough for the bird to stick its head through. If they are too large, the bird may strangle itself or get its head stuck because the lay of the feathers won't permit pulling the head back. If the spaces are large enough for the head to poke through easily, then the entire

17

# What a Mynah Needs to Thrive

body may slip through and the bird can get loose when you don't want it to be.

The bottom of the cage should consist of a drawer that you can pull out to clean. You can use bird sand as litter, spreading a layer that is not too thin because, as we mentioned earlier, mynahs produce not only wet droppings, but also great amounts of them. If the droppings are not absorbed by the litter, the bird ends up walking around in its own filth, which sticks to the toes and feet and is carried to all the perches and branches. However, bird sand is rather expensive, and you may want to substitute wrapping paper (not newspaper) with the matte side up because it is absorbent. If you use several layers, the paper will absorb the wetness well enough, though you will have to replace at least the top

You can construct a climbing tree for your mynah yourself. Drill a few holes in a short log, and stick some sturdy branches in the holes. Put the log with the branches in the center of a large tub, and fill up around the log with gravel and sand.

layers in the middle of the day and at night. Most aviculturists recommend that the cages of seed eaters be cleaned every day, and this advice is even more pertinent in the case of a soft-bill like the mynah. Mynahs have not only messy droppings but also messy eating habits. A mynah gets hold of a piece of fruit with its bill and chews on it while shaking its head back and forth vigorously in an attempt to reduce big chunks into bite-size morsels. Half the fruit goes flying through the air, some of it landing on the cage bars and the rest splattering on nearby walls and the floor. After about a week, the cage and the area around it look as though a bunch of savages had camped here. One way to avoid some of the messiness is to line the lower half of the cage, where the food dishes are, with glass or clear plastic. This at least reduces the amount of debris on the outside. As far as the inside of the cage goes, the best you can do is to wash it every day with hot water. It is of course true that some mynahs are messier than others. You'll soon be able to tell how often your mynah corner needs to be scrubbed. But it is always better to clean the cage too often than not often enough.

## Food and Water Dishes

You should have two food dishes—about the same size as those used for large parrots—so that fruit can be offered separately from other soft food (see page 39). The dishes should be mounted so that they are within easy reach of the perch. The

# What a Mynah Needs to Thrive

same is true for the water dish. Watch out that food and water dishes are not located where their contents might be contaminated by droppings. Don't mount them directly underneath perches. Place them in such a way that they can be filled from outside the cage. If you have to reach through the cage door every time your mynah needs more food or fresh water, your mynah will get upset, especially if he is just getting adjusted or if he is a shy bird. The water dish should not be too flat; the water has to be deep enough for the bird to be able to drink without having to go through any contortions (see page 41).

## The Perches

Ideally the perches should consist of unfinished wood and be of the right thickness. The bird should not be able to reach all the way around the wood with its three frontward pointing toes and one reverse toe; otherwise the claws don't get enough wear and may grow too long. Pet stores have plastic perches, which are easy to clean, but they are too smooth. The best perches for the birds are natural branches of different

Perches have to be thick enough so that the bird's toes do not touch when curling around them (left: correct; right: too thin).

thicknesses. This way the mynah has to continually adjust his grip just the way he does in nature. From time to time the branches have to be discarded and replaced with fresh ones. Swinging perches are not appropriate for mynahs. Rocking on them makes mynahs nervous, and a vacated swing can knock against the bird's head or back.

## The Nesting Cavity

In nature, mynahs breed in spherical hollows, and they also like to sleep in such cavities. If it is feasible, incorporate a starling nest box in the cage with a bedding of shavings, dried grasses, and twigs. Hang it on the outside of the cage with the entry hole facing in, so that the mynah can get into the nest from the cage. The inside dimensions should be about 8 x 8 x 8 inches (20 x 20 x 20 cm). The entry hole has to be large enough for the bird to be able to just fit through easily. A mynah will also make do with a semicircular hollow. If neither arrangement fits on or into your cage, your mynah may satisfy his need for cozy seclusion by disappearing underneath the wrapping paper on the cage floor when he gets ready to sleep. If that's what he wants, let him be. But if it becomes a habit, make sure that the paper is changed shortly before he retires for the night so that he doesn't have to slip under befouled bed covers.

So much for cages and their minimum size. But there are better ways of housing a mynah.

# What a Mynah Needs to Thrive

## Indoor Aviaries

An aviary offers room for flying; this will benefit the bird's health tremendously and significantly increase its life expectancy.

Basically an indoor aviary is simply a large cage, and everything I have said about cages also applies to aviaries. But there are a few more things to be said about aviaries. Indoor aviaries are commercially available, or they can be built to fit a specific space. The wire mesh used in an aviary should consist of wire encased by plastic. This way birds flying against the wire are not as likely to get hurt as when they crash against the sharp edges of plain galvanized wire. Also, the small doors and gates used in bird cages are inadequate for indoor aviaries. You need a regular door that allows you to enter the aviary. But keep the door size as small as is practicable in order to reduce chances of the bird's escaping when you open the door.

It is best to locate the aviary against a wall or in a corner of the room. The spot should be bright but not drafty. If the aviary is not too cumbersome you can mount it on rollers or wheels so that you can move it around. But move it gently; otherwise the motion may frighten your mynah.

An indoor aviary you could build yourself. It is large enough to house several different species of birds. Any aviary has to have plenty of securely mounted perches and branches. And don't forget to provide nesting facilities!

# What a Mynah Needs to Thrive

Another excellent indoor aviary is the bird room. This can be an extra room in the back of the house, an enclosed porch, etc. Building a bird room consists mostly of just installing wire screens in front of the windows and building a wire-mesh entrance hall inside the door.

Obviously, housing for mynahs and related species should be furnished to create as natural an effect as possible, such as that of an outdoor garden. The tiled or concrete floor should be sprinkled with sand that is replaced regularly. Try to maintain as much natural planting as possible, although the plants will have to be placed in pots and planters.

If perches and branches are not mounted very solidly, the bird's continual landings and take-offs will loosen them and perhaps cause them to fall. In an aviary, too, it is important to place food and water dishes within easy reach of perches. Never simply put them on the floor because the food and water will get dirty there in no time. One good solution is to put the dishes on a stand, which is then placed away from the perches. But be sure the stand has raised edges so that the dishes cannot be shoved off it. In an aviary the mynah should also be given a chance to take baths.

## Outdoor Aviaries

An outdoor aviary for mynahs can be set up on a balcony or in the garden. Mynahs are not much bothered by bad weather and can spend mild winters outdoors once they are acclimated. However, it is preferable and safer if your mynah has access to a sheltered room to which he can retreat during exceptionally cold weather or if the temperature stays below freezing for some time. My pet mynah Peter was fine at temperatures down to 23° F ($-10°$ C), but he was used to living outdoors from the beginning.

For readers who would like to house their mynah outdoors I should like to add a few remarks.

• If you have an outdoor aviary, watch out for predators and other harmful creatures, such as cats, martens, rats, and mice.

• Make sure the aviary can withstand the weight of a heavy snowfall. If there is any doubt, add extra supports for the roof.

• Check the wire mesh periodically for damage that might result in a hole through which the bird could escape.

An outdoor aviary that is not connected to an enclosed space always has to have a protected corner that is covered by a roof so that the birds have somewhere to retreat to during rainy weather or in other emergencies.

It is not worthwhile building a large outdoor aviary for a single mynah. In warm weather a single bird will be quite content if you take him out of his cage or indoor aviary and let him spend the day in a small outdoor aviary. But he should never be exposed to the wind or drafts, and he should be kept out of the direct sun. Of course you can also move his cage to the balcony for a few hours. But in that case, you have to make doubly sure that no cats are around that might reach between the bars of the cage and kill the bird. It is best if you make it a point to stay close by in such a situation.

# Basic Rules of Care

## Getting a Mynah Settled and Taming It

When you come home with your new mynah, everything should be ready for him. The cage or aviary should be set up and ready for its occupant, with the food and water dishes filled (see page 38).

### Acclimation after the Purchase

Remember that birds react badly to any change in environment and that they distrust anything new. If you have to change or arrange things in the cage after your mynah is already in it, you add to his distress by frightening him. This can have a lasting negative effect on the bird's relationship to you. And please don't reach your hand into the transport box to move him into the cage.

### Releasing the Bird into the Cage

Your bird was probably handed to you in a small cardboard box. As soon as you get home, get the box ready so that the top lifts up easily. It only has to open wide enough for the bird to be able to slip through the opening. If you then hold the opening against the open cage door, the bird will automatically move toward the light and hop from the box into the cage. Now close the cage door and stay around, standing or sitting down a few yards away. Don't stare at the bird continually, and if you have to move, do so slowly while talking to the bird softly and soothingly. When you see him shake his feathers and begin to preen himself, you'll know that he

is no longer petrified. Once he starts eating, the worst is over.

### Starting Out in a Cage or in an Aviary

If you have set up an outdoor aviary for your mynah, you should wait a little before releasing him there. Give him a chance to survey his new world for a few hours from a small cage first. Particularly if he is to move into an aviary with different kinds of birds in it, the newcomer should be given a chance to observe everything from a safe distance. Then he will find it easier to claim and defend a place of his own in the community.

Mynahs that have never lived outdoors and are used to having a protective ceiling over their heads should not be moved to an outdoor aviary from one day to the next. There are all kinds of alarming creatures flying through the air outdoors. Raptors are the natural enemies of all smaller birds, and a chicken hawk sailing through the sky above the garden, even if it has no designs on the mynah whatsoever, will trigger a fright reaction. In his panicked attempt to escape the danger the mynah may well get hurt. In time the mynah will learn that birds of prey cannot hurt him because they are kept out by the wire-mesh top of the aviary. (At night, however, mynahs never lose their fear of owls.) Even airplanes can evoke fear because, to an inexperienced mynah, they appear like outsized raptors. The fact that birds of prey are silent and do not rumble like airplanes is beside the point because birds rely on their eyesight for clues, not on their ears.

Many years ago, at my parents' house in

Munich, West Germany, which was situated directly beneath a flight lane to the airport, I kept a tame curlew in the garden. At first he flattened himself in the grass every time a plane arrived or took off. After a few days he simply crouched down, and after some more time he merely pulled his head in, until he finally ignored the planes altogether. Remember to give your bird time to adjust. Give him an opportunity to get acquainted through a window with what's going on in the world outside before setting him loose in the aviary.

But let's get back to the mynah in his cage. When he seems relaxed and content after a few hours, you can start going about your normal business. Still, avoid abrupt movements and loud, startling noises. Cover the cage on two or three sides with a light cloth in the evening. This will make the bird feel safer. However, if he seems frightened when you approach with the cover, don't bother with it. Perhaps the bird will get used to it later. It is not absolutely necessary to cover the bird at night, though many like it and even miss it if you fail to do it one night.

## The First Hours

No matter what kind of housing you have for your mynah, give him at least a few hours to get adjusted to it. Don't put him in his cage or aviary just before dark or at night when he has no chance to get oriented. This applies particularly to aviaries because a bird feels more confused in a larger space than in a more surveyable cage. In an outdoor aviary he might inadvertently choose an inappropriate spot to spend the night, where he is not protected from the elements. The next morning you might find him soaked and chilled to the bone, perhaps even dead.

## Getting Used to the Hand

If it is important to you to have a mynah that quickly becomes friendly enough to be hand-tamed—which means that the bird comes to your hand or shoulder of his own volition—a cage is better than a large outdoor aviary. In the latter the bird can always get away from you, and it is difficult to get close without scaring him away. In a cage, however, he has to put up with your proximity whether he likes it or not. This may sound like a harsh method, but it does speed up the process of getting acquainted. Perhaps you have wondered on occasion how little the birds (and other animals) in zoological gardens are bothered by the thousands of visitors that stream by their cages. The answer is simply that they have gotten used to the crowds and no longer pay any attention. In large aviaries and enclosed outdoor areas, however, the birds are usually to be found on the far side of the enclosure.

If your mynah came straight from the nest, he will get used to your hand quite naturally because it is the source of food. Such a bird never develops a fear of the hand. Let him sit on your hand as soon as he leaves his artificial nest (see page 50). From that point on everything happens automatically. As long as a bird has no bad experiences with a human hand he will not shun it.

# Basic Rules of Care

## Giving Treats

Older mynahs may shy away from human hands at first. The best way to overcome this reluctance is to offer your bird treats. But first he should be given plenty of time to get used to his new home. As soon as you can stand in front of the cage without his displaying any sign of fear you can show him a treat, perhaps a mealworm that you hold between your fingers or let wriggle on the palm of your hand. The mynah will eye it with great interest but not yet reach for it. Let the mealworm wriggle around for a minute or so and then put it in the cage or the food dish where the mynah can get it. Do this for a few days, getting a little closer to the bird every time, and eventually the bird will take the food with extended neck and flattened feathers. Now you've won the game. Keep offering food until the mynah

Even when your mynah is quite at ease on your hand you still should avoid sudden and abrupt movements so that your pet will not lose his balance.

yanks the worm out of your hand without a moment's hesitation.

## How to Lure the Mynah onto Your Hand

When the mynah has gotten used to your hand as a source of food, open the cage door and slowly move the hand with the treat into the cage. If the mynah is not frightened, proceed as follows: Hold your left hand in front of the bird about level with his belly. Now, with your right hand, hold the worm out toward the bird. To grab the worm, the mynah will have to hop onto your left hand. Keep your hands very still now, and be sure not to pull the hand with the mynah on it out of the cage. You can't do that until the bird has really settled on the hand because, in most cases, he has to bend down or go through some sort of contortions to fit through the door. Once you are able to get your hand with the bird on it out of the cage, there is nothing more to it. The only thing to remember is never to move your hand abruptly or jerkily while the mynah is perched on it. That would upset his physical as well as his mental equilibrium.

## Can a Mynah Be Housebroken?

Trying to housebreak a mynah is a hopeless enterprise. This is true for birds in general. Their digestion is too rapid and practically continuous, and excretion is not in any way associated with other behavior. Mammals are different in this respect. A dog marks his territory with his urine and bowels, and he picks certain spots to do this. He automatically gets used to these spots and easily learns where he may and may not relieve himself. A bird would never learn this, and punishment is completely useless.

The only bird I ever knew to become partially housebroken, or rather "shoulder-broken," belonged to my father. It was a cockatiel that somehow did learn that he was allowed to leave his cage only after he had produced some droppings. My father taught him this with infinite patience by standing in front of the cage, saying over and over, "Do your duty!" First the bird would comply occasionally by sheer coincidence, upon which he was instantly "rewarded" by being let out. Eventually he visibly strained to produce a dropping when he was asked to. There was no telling when the next dropping would come, and we had to put him back into the cage every twenty minutes and ask him to repeat his performance if we wanted our shoulders or the table to stay relatively clean. But you could never teach this trick to a mynah.

## Water Baths and Sand Baths

Mynahs like to take frequent baths, and when they do they make the water fly. That is why you should not put a bathtub in a small cage. Otherwise you'll have to dry everything from top to bottom. In an aviary you should place the bathtub the same way you do the food and water dishes: Set it on a board on top of a stand (see page 19). If your mynah is tame and comes to your hand or has a daily free flying session, you can let him have his bath around noon outside the cage.

A clay saucer for a flowerpot makes a good bathtub. It should be large enough for the entire bird to fit into it without unnatural bending of the neck. Neither should the tail stick out over the edge, because it is in special need of cleaning. Flowerpot saucers and other flat dishes tend to have smooth surfaces on which the bird's feet slip easily. This is a frightening experience, especially for a bird that is not yet accustomed to such artificial puddles. If you have bought your mynah from a pet dealer and it is a "gaper" or youngster (see page 44), you may safely assume that it has never yet bathed. The small cages in which these creatures spend their time until they are bought offer no opportunity for bathing. The most the birds can do is to dip their bills in the drinking water and splash a little of it over themselves. But that is not a proper mynah bath. Bathing to a mynah means stepping into water up to the belly, flapping his wings wildly, sticking his head underwater, crouching down, and getting wet all over from the splashing water. A mynah will go through these motions over and over, sometimes for several minutes, until the tub is empty and the bird thoroughly soaked. Then the drying off, preening, and smoothing of the feathers begins. To prevent the bird slipping in the bathtub, you can place a thin layer of foam rubber or a piece of felt in the bottom. This will provide the bird's feet with a grip and prevent accidents.

A mynah's sense of well-being will be much enhanced by a daily bath in wrist warm water (in the summer it can be cooler but never ice cold).

I read in a book on birds that mynahs

also like to take dust or sand baths. This may be so, but I've never observed this behavior in my mynahs, although there was plenty of sand and dirt in their outside aviaries. You can give it a try with your bird. Give him a bowl of dry, clean sand that is warmed through by the sun and see what he does.

## Trimming Overgrown Claws

Sometimes the horny part of the bill and the claws grows too long in a bird that lives in captivity, interfering with the intake of food as well as with other movements. The reasons for this are insufficient use of the bill and perches that are too thin to supply enough wear of the toenails.

Overgrowth of the upper beak is quite rare in mynahs. (This condition is more common in parrots and parakeets, which need to do a lot of cracking and rasping work with their bills.) The toenails are more likely to get too long, but it is quite

How to trim overgrown toenails properly: Take the bird in your left hand, secure his head between your index and middle fingers, and hold his leg with your middle and ring fingers. Then quickly trim the claws to proper length with sharp, small wire cutters.

Cutting the nails: The drawing on the left shows the wrong way; the one on the right, the right way. Make sure you don't cut into the quick.

easy to cure this problem. Take the bird in your left hand as depicted in the drawing in the left-hand column. Hold his head between your index and middle finger, keeping the bird from slipping out of your grip head first. Now hold the leg with the nails to be trimmed firmly with your middle and ring fingers. Take small, sharp wire nippers and snip off the end of the nail. If you cut too close to the toe, you may cause bleeding, because a blood vessel extends into the base of the nail. In light-colored claws, this blood vessel is visible as a dark shadow when the toe is held up against the light. Cut a few millimeters in front of this shadow (see drawing this page). If there should be slight bleeding, this will not really harm the bird. It will stop soon. If cutting seems too risky to you, you can file the nails down, but this takes longer.

## Clipping Wings

When aviculturists speak of clipping a bird's wings, they mean shortening some flight feathers on one side only, which will

The exceptional flexibility of a mynah's neck comes in handy when the bird preens his feathers.

leave the bird unable to fly until the next molt. It is a procedure that is *not recommended* for mynahs because these birds crash hard to the floor when they try to fly. This can cause not only fractures but also other potentially fatal injuries. What's more, mynahs that are deprived of flying tend to grow obese. Even if you clip just enough feathers off one wing to reduce the bird's agility without depriving him of flight altogether, this will make him clumsy, interfere with his flight maneuvers, and force him to land where he didn't intend to. The consequences here, too, may be a crash to the floor and injuries.

## Flying Free Indoors and Other Dangers

You may be puzzled why I mention free flying in the same breath with dangers. But you'll find out in a moment all the misfortunes that can befall a mynah. I think it would be fair to say that more pet birds die as a result of accidents than because of illness or senility.

### Watch Out During the Daily Free Flying
It is your responsibility to try to prevent all conceivable accidents. But no matter how cautious you are and even when you think you have foreseen all possibilities, something can still go wrong. In the course of the many years during which I've kept birds I've seen accidents arise from the

Dangers lurking in the kitchen. Hot burners and pots can spell disaster.

most unsuspected circumstances, and I think I've learned from these experiences. But there still are always surprises. However, let me list the most common dangers.

Feathers should not be clipped until they are fully grown and the blood has receded from the quill.

In order to stay fit, your mynah should be able to fly free in your apartment or house every day if at all possible. But when you first acquire the bird he should stay locked in his cage for about two weeks to get used to his new home and to you. The tamer he is, the less prone he will be to accidents on his first venture out of the cage. Even after that he will always be more easily frightened in new surroundings than in his accustomed setting (and any place outside the cage represents an unfamiliar environment to him). Before you let your mynah out of his cage for the first time, mount a few branches in various spots in the upper half of the room to serve as secure perches. Most of our furniture, with the possible exception of upholstered chair backs, offers poor landing opportunities for bird feet. The wood is too smooth, and a bird can easily slip on a cabinet or bookcase and end up between the piece of furniture and the wall. There he is stuck and unable to scramble out. If you happen to be around you can extricate him, but if not, he is in a bad way.

### Flying Against a Window

Before opening the cage door to let your mynah stretch his wings, make sure all the windows and doors are closed. Pull curtains or drapes or let down Venetian blinds at all the windows because birds are attracted by light. A mynah emerging from his cage will head directly or after a few moments for a window and most likely bump into it. If he is flying slowly he will merely slide down the glass and flutter on. But if he has gathered speed he may bump hard enough to suffer a concussion. If this should happen to your bird, place

If a mynah crashes into an unprotected window he may sustain a concussion—or possibly break his neck.

him in a warm, dark spot, where he will probably recover after a while. If he crashes into the window at full tilt the likely outcome is a broken neck or fractured skull, which means death. Closed drapes or some other window covers eliminate this risk. If a mynah survives a minor collision with a window he usually learns to watch out and will later fly against such an invisible barrier only in a state of extreme panic. But that first encounter might be deadly. That is why I urge you to provide and close curtains or shutters or whatever before you let your bird out of his cage for the first time. During the summer months you can substitute a window screen for the drapes so that you can still air the room while the bird is flying loose.

### Escape

Occasionally mynahs manage to find a way to escape. You might have forgotten to shut a window, and before you know it your mynah is sitting on a tree branch outside. What happens now depends primarily on how tame your bird is. If he is shy, the chances of recapturing him are practically nil, because something in the wide world of the outside is bound to frighten him and make him fly away. You'll soon lose sight of him, and then there is nothing you can do to recover him. A tame mynah is more likely to stay in the immediate environs, and when he gets hungry he'll respond to the call of your familiar voice. You can also try putting his cage outside in the hope that he'll return to his familiar home and the food inside it. Whatever you do, avoid loud calling and nervous running around, as well as the presence of unfamiliar people. All these things would alarm your mynah and prevent him from returning.

A mynah that has escaped from an outdoor aviary in which he has lived for some time will probably stay nearby as long as nothing drives him too far away. Here, too, hunger is likely to motivate a voluntary return. Often tame birds that have escaped will let their keeper come quite close but are too upset to come to his hand or shoulder. For such moments you should have a bird net (see drawing in right-hand column) to whip over the bird's head. Your aim has to be accurate, however, for if you do not succeed at the first or at most the second try, the bird will be so suspicious of the contraption that any further attempts at capture will be hopeless.

What is of paramount importance when a bird has escaped is not to let him out of sight. You wouldn't believe how difficult it is to find him again once he has disappeared into the thick foliage of a tree. And since he is frightened out of his wits, he will probably not make a sound, thus depriving you of the clue his voice could provide.

To sum it all up: Preventing possible escapes by conscientiously closing windows is a lot easier than trying to catch a bird on the loose.

Of course I, too, once let a tame mynah get away. I say "of course" because it would be practically unheard of for someone to own a tame bird for almost ten years without some such incident. My mynah Peter lived in an outdoor aviary, and one

morning when I came to feed him he escaped. This was not very difficult for him because I had forgotten to close the door behind me. (This kind of thing usually happens to me in the morning because it takes me a good hour to wake up completely after I get up.) In any case, Peter flew through the open door and made for the topmost branch of a nearby pear tree. There he sang happily. I was not particularly upset because my wife was in the house, and I knew she would take care of the matter and somehow lure the bird back. So I told her that we had a mynah flying free in the garden, that he was presently perched on the pear tree, that I was off to work, and that I would appreciate it if she would turn her attention to the problem.

The best way to retrieve your escaped mynah is to use a bird net, but you have to hit the mark by the second try at the latest!

She did turn her attention to the problem, and, as I found out when I came home after work, it took her almost the entire day to get Peter back in his aviary. It

# Basic Rules of Care

seems that he had recently eaten his fill, which made recapturing him more of a challenge. It is relatively easy to lure and catch a hungry bird, but a sated one wants to have a good look at the world before he considers returning to captivity. Luckily nothing happened to cause headlong flight. No low-flying airplane passed overhead, and no wild bird defending his territory scared Peter away.

Still, Peter turned a deaf ear to my wife's calling and cajoling in the sweetest tones she knew. She offered him mealworms—his favorite treat—on the palm of her hand and scattered on the ground. About five dollars worth of mealworms wriggled away in all directions and gradually out of sight without eliciting any sign of interest in the recalcitrant bird. After two hours, my wife went back inside to work. Some time later she came out again to look for Peter, but he was nowhere to be seen. Whistling and calling, she searched all around the house but found nothing—which is not too surprising. You try sometime to find a bird the size of a mynah sitting silently in the thick leaves of a summery tree.

Around noon a neighbor came running to report that a small crow with a yellow bill was sitting on his balcony. Could that be our bird? Yes, my wife answered, that was no doubt our mynah which she had been hunting for hours. Would he mind if she came over to catch it? That was fine with the neighbor but not with Peter. As soon as she appeared on the balcony he flew onto the roof. There he was hidden from her view, and she went down to the street to see him. Peter promptly flew back to the balcony. This game continued for some time. Because our neighbor had several cats, my wife was worried about Peter's safety, and she went up and down more often than she would have otherwise. But finally she gave up, leaving Peter sitting wherever he wished, and asked the neighbor to call her if anything new developed. I called home in the course of the afternoon to ask how things stood with Peter, but the only answer I got was some language unfit for print and the information that a sinkful of dirty dishes was awaiting my return.

Hunger got the better of Peter in the end. He reappeared on the roof of his aviary, hopped around restlessly for a while, and made straight for my wife's hand when she—having become aware of him—went out with a bowl of fruit. He let himself be taken into the aviary without any objection, gorged himself, and acted as though nothing special had happened. When I came home from work, I was of course much relieved to find Peter back where he belonged. And I have taken to heart the suggestion that I not feed my birds until I am fully awake.

**Burns and Electric Shocks**

A mynah has no way of knowing that an electric burner that has just been turned off is still hot or that a toaster that is working carries electricity. If he happens to land on such an appliance he may get burned or sustain an electric shock. Electric heaters belong in this category, too. He may not even want to land on a heater, but the

# *Basic Rules of Care*

glowing red wires may tempt him to peck at them. So check to make sure all dangerous appliances are turned off or out of the bird's reach before you let him out of his cage.

Electric wires can be deadly! Always make sure there is no chance for your bird to get at them.

### Other Dangers

Human habitations contain more dangers than the ones already mentioned. Large vases or any other uncovered containers with water in them have spelled doom for many a bird. Trying to take a bath or drink from such a container, a mynah may lose his balance on the smooth edge, fall in the water, be unable to climb out, and drown.

Mynahs that are very tame and want to accompany their keepers everywhere are exposed to risk precisely because of their wish to stay close to people. If you leave the mynah's room and close the door behind you without checking to see if your feathered friend is following you, he can easily get squashed in the door. Or if he hops along behind you or comes to meet you, you may accidently step on him. Be sure to tell visitors as soon as they arrive that your pet bird is flying loose at the moment. If taken by surprise by a flying bird, many people wave their arms in automatic self-defense and may hit the bird by mistake. A tumble to the ground is of relatively minor consequence.

Let me mention one more source of accidents: sewing and knitting materials. Birds are intrigued by loops and tangles of thread or yarn and try to play with them. They want to see whether the stuff is edible or whether it could be used for building nests, and before you know it the neck is caught in a noose, and the poor bird hangs himself.

**Remember:** As long as you stay in the room where your mynah is flying loose, he is quite safe because you can keep an eye on him. Try not to leave him alone or, if you must, only for a moment. This is the best way to avoid all kinds of disaster.

Hot range tops are a menace!

# Basic Rules of Care

## List of Dangers

| Source of Danger | Effect |
| --- | --- |
| Windows, glass doors, glass walls. | Collision, causing concussion, fractured skull, or broken neck. |
| Doors; windows or doors left open. | Getting squashed; escaping. |
| Stoves, radiators, toasters, etc. | Burns. |
| Electric wires and outlets. | Electric shocks. |
| Vases, pots, pails or other containers full of water. | Drowning. |
| Bathtubs and sinks. | Drowning. |
| Crocheted and knitted items. | Getting claws caught; hanging to death. |
| Knitting yarn, string, and sewing thread. | Getting caught in loops and strangling. |
| Spaces between furniture and walls. | Sliding down and getting stuck. |
| Hard floors. | Birds that have not yet fully mastered flying suffer fractured legs or wings and bruises when crashing down. |
| Improper size of wire mesh in aviaries or wrong spacing of bars in cages or aviaries. | Sticking head through, getting it stuck, and choking to death. |
| Mesh made of wire that is too thin and sharp. | Injuries on head and toes. |
| Perches that are too thin. | Overgrown toenails. |
| Rusted wires or holes in mesh of aviary. | Escaping. |
| Open pipes or pipelike cavities. | Slipping in, getting stuck, suffocating. Birds breeding in tree holes seek out such retreats and are then often unable to extricate themselves without help. |
| Sharp ends of wire, nails, wood splinters. | Puncture wounds and scratches. |
| Perches and branches not mounted securely enough. | Fractures; being hit by falling branch. |
| Human feet. | Being stepped on. |

# Basic Rules of Care

## Children and Mynahs

Children, especially very young ones, have no idea how easily a mynah is frightened. If a child comes up to the cage full of interest and good intentions and runs his toy car across the cage bars or simply approaches too quickly in a burst of excitement, this can send the bird into a frenzied panic. Keep this in mind. The bird may "punish" the intruding child, and all hope of friendship will be over for good. Or the child may respond with terror if the bird gives a sharp nip to small fingers held out in tentative friendship or suddenly lands on the child's shoulder with wild fluttering and loud screeching. In general, however, children love mynahs. I don't know how many children I have seen convulsed with laughter or with faces transfixed with amazement when a mynah produced his store of imitations with deceptive accuracy. After a while you'll know your bird well enough to judge whether or not you should allow him to land on the shoulders or hands of children. In general, you should always observe the following rules when you introduce a bird to a child (the same applies for all kinds of small pets): Proceed with caution, make sure everybody is calm, watch carefully how both parties react, and if the bird seems upset, remove the source of his agitation.

## Mynahs and Other Pets

In most combinations of household pets, birds like mynahs are the smaller and therefore the more vulnerable party. It is hardly necessary to point out that dogs and cats in the same household represent a danger for birds.

### A Dog and a Mynah

If you think your dog will show no interest in a mynah, he would have to be an exceptional canine indeed, not only good-natured but also docile to the point of obeying your every word. By showing interest I mean snapping at a bird that is hopping around disrespectfully in front of the dog's nose or alighting on his back or head. But you're the best judge of what your dog will put up with. If you bring home a mynah, introduce the two pets to each other gradually. The mynah will be afraid of the dog at first, and the dog will probably feel jealous. As long as the mynah is in his cage, he is relatively safe. I say relatively because a big dog could knock over even a fairly large cage, and in the process the door might open and the bird escape. Now he might be easy prey for the dog. Teach your dog from the first that the bird is a "no-no," but keep petting him to let him know you still love him. A normal dog will gradually accept the newcomer and eventually lose interest in him. But, as I said, this is true only as long as the bird is confined to the cage. When he is loose, it's a different story. A flying bird awakens the dog's hunting instinct, and the dog may snap at the moving prey when you least suspect it. So never leave a bird and dog alone in a room unless the two have really made friends. The same applies to cats, except that you have to be even more careful.

# Basic Rules of Care

## Cats, Rabbits, and Guinea Pigs

Cats that leave birds alone are practically unheard of. But perhaps you have pet rabbits or guinea pigs. Don't assume that these animals are harmless. I once saw a male rabbit attack a tame jackdaw, which he would have killed if I had not been there to intervene. Guinea pigs, too, bite—sometimes out of fear, or because they're startled, or simply to defend their territory. As a rule mynahs are smart enough to avoid the danger of being attacked and instinctively keep at a safe distance from dogs, cats, and other mammals. But if they've been raised in captivity along with other pets, they may be so used to these household companions that they have lost their natural fear of unfamiliar animals. In cases like this accidents do occur with some frequency.

## Mynahs and Other Birds Together in One Aviary

### Mixed Communities

I never had any trouble keeping mynahs—and I have had five or six of them over the years—together with other birds in my aviaries. Most aviaries are large enough for their inhabitants to avoid each other if they wish (see "Starting Out in a Cage or in an Aviary," page 22). Also, mynahs are relatively peaceful members of the bird kingdom. Still, they can do considerable harm to the nestlings of smaller species, sometimes even killing them.

### Mynahs May Harm Smaller Birds

If small birds like canaries raise young in an aviary that contains a mynah, it does happen that the latter eats the nestlings. Even the nest or eggs will be much the worse for wear if the mynah decides to take an interest in them.

Don't put a mynah in a smallish cage with considerably smaller birds. The mere presence of the larger bird will make the smaller species nervous, and there is always the possibility that the mynah might go after one of the little birds and kill it.

### More Than One Mynah in an Aviary or Cage

There is no need to worry about anything in the case of a community of mynahs. As far as my own experience goes, a new mynah can join an already established group in an outdoor aviary without any problems. Either the birds ignore each other, or they make friends sooner or later. Since mynahs live communally in the wild, they generally adopt the same life style in an aviary. If you want to combine two mynahs in an indoor cage, keep them in separate cages for a while at first to give them a chance to get used to each other.

## When You Go Away

If you are going away and will be gone for some time, you'll have to decide beforehand what to do with your mynah. Birds are attached to their familiar surroundings and don't care about vacations.

# Basic Rules of Care

You have only two choices: Either you take your mynah with you, or you leave him at home.

## Arranging for Care During Your Absence

If you leave your mynah at home, you have to find someone to look after him. The caretaker has to be reliable and willing to do more than the bare essentials. A mynah that is used to spending most of his time with you will naturally be unhappy if the person looking after him appears only once a day to supply food and clean the cage and then leaves again. There is nothing worse for an affectionate bird than being abandoned by the human he is attached to and sitting alone in his cage for weeks.

If you cannot find anybody willing to spend a lot of time with your mynah in your home, it is better to move the bird, cage and all, to someone else's house. He will quickly get used to the new people and the new surroundings as long as he stays in his own familiar cage. Of course you have to leave precise instructions describing how you tend to your mynah's needs, how you talk to him, what he likes, and what annoys him. If his daily life follows the routine he is used to, this will help him get over the separation from you.

## Vacationing with a Mynah

If you want to and are able to take your mynah along on a trip, this makes sense only if you spend your vacation in one place. Sleeping in a different motel every night is the last thing a mynah would enjoy. If your mynah is transported without his cage, a cage that is similar in size and general setup to the one at home should await him at the point of destination. If this is impossible, you'll have to follow the same procedures as described for introducing a bird to his new home after purchase (see page 22).

The trip itself, whether by car or other transportation, is inevitably a stressful experience for a mynah. If your car is large enough you may be able to fit the bird's cage into it. If not, you'll have to pack him in a small box or crate for the trip (never a plastic container!). This will be adequate for a few hours. The container has to have a lot of small holes to let in enough air but not much light. The bird will be calmer in the dark. Don't think that your bird will enjoy looking out of the car window. Seeing the scenery flash by will only agitate him. That is also why you should drape a cloth over the cage for a trip. One of the most important things is to check that your mynah is not too warm. Never leave him in a closed car that is parked in the sun. And, of course, the mynah has to be able to eat and drink at least every couple of hours. Stop in a quiet spot, uncover the cage, check to make sure everything is in order, and give the bird a chance to recover for a while.

## Travel to Other States and Abroad

Ordinarily, traveling with a mynah presents no major problems. Most foreign countries, however, require an official health certificate for pet birds and poultry, certifying that the birds are free of contagious diseases.

# *Basic Rules of Care*

Often, quarantining your bird(s) for a certain period is required. This period can last from one day to six months or longer. If you want to be on the safe side, get in touch with the appropriate consulate several weeks before your planned trip to find out whether you need a health certificate for your mynah. Regulations vary from country to country. Also find out what laws govern the reentry of birds into the United States. And think up a good explanation ahead of time in case your mynah, when uncovered by an official, decides to shout some unflattering remark at him.

# The Right Diet

## How and What Mynahs Eat

I have already mentioned that mynahs are soft-bills. As such, they live primarily on fruit of all kinds. They also eat insects and, occasionally, small vertebrates. But they don't like seeds. They pick up the food they want to eat with their strong bills. If the morsel is too big to be swallowed, a mynah tries to get a bite-sized piece off by chomping on it with his bill and shaking his head. When the piece is reduced to the right size, it is tossed back into the gullet and gulped down as is. It is quite amazing how wide the beak and esophagus will open and what size morsel they can accommodate. A whole cherry goes down without the slightest difficulty. And you don't have to worry that the bird might choke. Food that is troublesome is quickly regurgitated and cut down to size or rearranged so it slides down more easily.

Mynahs are soft-bills, that is, they eat only soft foods. They often have extremely sloppy eating habits, which necessitate thorough daily cleaning of the cage and its surroundings.

## Fruit and Insects to Feed

Fruit contains a lot of water and a small amount of indigestible fiber, and it does not have much food value. Insects (for the average mynah owner this means mostly mealworms, which are the larvae of various beetles of the family Tenebrionidae) are very nutritious, since they are rich in fats. Mealworms are available at pet stores. But feeding too many of them may be harmful because they contain chitin, an indigestible substance. Offering mealworms three times a week is plenty. Mealworms are also quite expensive. A mynah doesn't have to have them as a daily staple, and they can be saved for special treats. A mynah that is kept in an outdoor aviary will catch some insects for himself. If your mynah lives almost entirely on fruit, he will consume great amounts of it. You can offer him all sorts: bananas, cherries, grapes; chopped apple, pear, or melon; strawberries, raspberries, juniper berries, rowan berries, gooseberries, to mention just some possibilities. All of these can be given in generous amounts, but they will pass through the digestive tract quickly and they are not highly nutritious. That is why we have to try to supply a substitute for the insects and small vertebrates the birds would eat in nature. A bird that is fed nothing but fruit will sooner or later show symptoms of nutritional deficiencies. Low-fat cottage cheese and/or strips of lean meat are good protein foods. Beef heart is also excellent. Chopped beef—but without any fat—is easily digested and is popular with mynahs. Fat should always be avoided because it makes the bird fat.

# The Right Diet

## A Mixture to Serve as the Basic Staple

I have come up with the following recipe for my mynahs. The recipe can be used for the birds' basic meals, and I have had excellent success with it for many years. Take:

  1 pound of low-fat cottage cheese
  2 bananas
  2 handfuls of uncooked oatmeal
  2 handfuls of commercial bird food for soft-bills (available from pet stores).

Mix everything together in a bowl and knead well. The mixture should have the consistency of pie-crust dough. If it is too wet and sticks to your fingers, there is too much banana or cottage cheese and you have to add some more oatmeal. If it crumbles apart when you knead it, it is too dry and needs some extra cottage cheese or banana.

When you have finished kneading, form the mixture into balls about the size of a small apple. The recipe will yield about four or five balls, and your mynah will go through about one a day, eating some of it and wasting the rest with his head-shaking. Put the other balls away in the refrigerator, covered or wrapped in foil to keep them from drying out. This way you can prepare your bird's food all at once for four or five days. That is one advantage. You can also vary the daily menu by adding various ingredients, such as small amounts of honey or some organically grown raisins (available at health food stores), or you can add vitamins and bird calcium. Another variation is to substitute other fruit (also organically raised, of course) for some or all the banana.

## Mynahs Need a Varied Diet

Varying the diet is always a good idea. I give my mynahs the mixture described above and *in addition* supply different fresh fruit in a separate dish.

Try giving your mynah some straight meat and see how he likes it. Not every mynah eats everything. The culinary taste of a bird is often shaped or determined by the foods he was reared on or by what he was fed before you bought him. It won't take much time to discover what appeals to his palate and what gets discarded. Then you simply omit the latter.

## Amounts of Food

A number of factors affect how much food you may or should give your mynah. Birds that fly a lot, either outside their cage or in a large aviary, eat more than ones that are confined to a small cage. Java Hill Mynahs need more than their smaller

Plastic dishes like this one are suitable for food as well as water and can be hung anywhere on the cage grating.

# The Right Diet

cousins, the Lesser India Hill Mynahs. If you give more fruit than foods high in fat and protein, you'll have to supply larger portions. I have already mentioned a ball of my special concoction as an average daily feeding. That was designed for mynahs living in an outdoor aviary. I can't give you any more precise instructions about how much to feed your bird. You'll just have to watch him. If there are leftovers, you're being too generous. Cut down on the basic mixture and make up for it with more fruit. No mynah overeats or gets fat on fruit. If, on the other hand, the dish is empty by midday, the mynah's restless search for food will indicate pretty clearly that he is still hungry.

## Commercial Mynah Food— But Not as an Exclusive Diet

Pet-supply stores now sell a commercial mynah food in the form of pellets similar to the ones that have been available for

A water dispenser suitable for a mynah cage. The dish at the bottom is deep enough for the bird to be able to immerse his entire bill and pick up water comfortably.

some time for various other small animals. This can be used as a supplement to the basic diet, and it is said to make the mynah's droppings more solid. But I wouldn't recommend it as an exclusive diet. Feeding a mynah nothing but pellet food would be equivalent to our living on artificially flavored pills instead of eating meat and potatoes and all the other good things we enjoy. Let me repeat once more: Variety and frequent changes in diet are always beneficial!

## Drinking Water

Mynahs like to drink water and do so frequently. Make sure the water dish is always clean and filled with fresh water. If necessary, change the water several times a day. By the way, bird vitamins can be added to the food or drinking water. They are needed only in very small amounts, but are essential for normal development, growth, and maintenance of good health. Without vitamins, the utilization of fat, protein, and carbohydrates would be impossible. Because birds have rapid metabolism, vitamin supplements are essential to their health. There are various bird vitamins available. However, you should avoid vitamin preparations designed for humans.

# Raising Mynahs

Although mynahs are now kept by many fanciers and in almost all zoos, they rarely reproduce in captivity. The first viable offspring of captive mynahs were born in 1957 on the Kerton Farm in England. We know very little about what conditions are necessary for these birds to mate, or even about the details of the mating process. It seems strange that these friendly and tame birds should be so reluctant to raise young in captivity, though I have a hunch that the cause may be related precisely to their adaptibility to humans.

We know that many birds—as well as mammals—that are raised by humans refuse to establish normal bonds with their fellows. They regard their human partner as a member of their own species and reject potential mates of their own kind. Ethologists express this by saying that such animals are imprinted to humans. This imprinting may well be one reason for the lack of offspring of tame mynahs.

## The Difficulties of Sexing Mynahs

Obviously you have to have a pair of birds, i.e., a male and a female, if you hope for offspring. But since males and females are indistinguishable in appearance and since two birds of the same sex often behave just like a true pair, ending up with two birds capable of raising a family may be more a matter of luck than planning.

I had owned my mynah Peter for eight years without having any idea what sex he was when I acquired a second bird that looked exactly like Peter. The only way I could tell them apart was that Peter talked and the other bird did not. The two lived in the same aviary, but they did not seem inordinately fond of each other. The newcomer was rather shy, and as soon as anybody approached the aviary, he withdrew into the farthest corner.

Male and female mynahs are look-alikes; there are no external sex differences. And don't be fooled by their behavior: Two birds of the same gender often behave like a true pair.

You can imagine my surprise when some time in June I discovered eggs in one of the nest boxes. The eggs were warm, so they were obviously not abandoned. By watching unobtrusively, I found out that both Peter and the new mynah took turns sitting on the eggs. Peter, in fact, became quite aggressive and made for my head and hands whenever I got too close to the nest box, nipping me quite painfully a few times. The two birds produced several more clutches over time, but I never was able to figure out which of them actually laid the eggs. All of the eggs were infertile, so I probably had two females. Also, I understand that mynahs generally lay only two or three eggs per clutch while I usually found four or five in a box. Presumably both females were laying and took turns sitting. Needless to say, the eggs did not hatch, and my initial wild hope for baby mynahs went unfulfilled.

## What You Would Need for Raising Mynahs

Still, if you have several mynahs in an aviary you might want to set up conditions conducive to breeding. In such a case you need to know as much as possible about the process of reproduction and watch for signs.

Mynahs breed in cavities (see page 19) and need the right kind of nest box for their eggs. (Even if they don't have eggs, they like nest boxes to sleep in at night.) The interior of a nest box for mynahs should measure about 8 by 8 by 8 inches (20 x 20 x 20 cm). The entry hole should accommodate the individual bird, being just large enough for him to fit through. You also have to give some thought to the location of the nest box. Hang it as high up as you can under a roof that keeps out the rain, and orient the entry hole away from the quarter where most of the rain and wind originates in your locality.

### What Is the Best Kind of Nest Box?
Nowadays artificial nesting cavities made of pressed wood are available for all sizes

of birds. Pressed wood is preferable to regular wood (which you can, of course, use to build nest boxes yourself) because it is more durable. Also, the inside of the nest is easier to clean, and there are less crannies for parasites to hide in (see page 59).

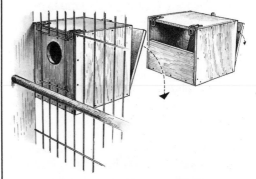

An ideal nest box: The inside dimensions should be at least 8 by 8 by 8 inches (20 x 20 x 20 cm). The entry hole has to be large enough for the mynah to enter and exit easily. Notice that the back wall flips open. This is a very practical feature.

Avoid nest boxes made of plastic. They overheat in the summer and are too cold in the winter. Pressed wood, on the other hand, acts as an insulator at all times of year. The commercially available nest boxes of pressed wood are not designed for mynahs but for wild birds instead. The entry holes of nest boxes for starlings are too small for the Greater India and the Java Hill Mynahs. These boxes can be used only for the Lesser India Hill Mynah. But the nest boxes intended for kestrels and stock doves are adequate for the two larger varieties of mynahs. Nest boxes of this kind can be purchased at or ordered from many garden supply companies, pet stores, or societies for the protection of birds.

My mynahs had the messy habit of depositing their droppings inside the box during the night. That meant that the box had to be scrubbed thoroughly from time to time to keep the birds' plumage relatively clean. Watch out for this problem.

### The Right Nesting Materials

Most members of the starling family build untidy and large nests if they have enough room. A nest is not much more than a tangled heap of grass, hay, and leaves. My two mynahs used small twigs as nesting material, some of which were so stiff that they caused the eggs to break. When I became aware of this, I myself padded the nest with hay and put the eggs back in. This goes to show that you have to make sure there is adequate nesting material available and lend a helping hand if your mynah doesn't do the job properly.

## Brooding—Hatching— Raising Baby Mynahs

I cannot tell you what the incubation period for mynah eggs is, but I would guess that it is between 14 and 18 days. You can be quite sure that nothing will come of eggs that have been incubated more than 20 days. Try to avoid bothering birds that are incubating eggs. Restrain your curiosity, and check the nest no more often than once every two or three days, and then preferably when no bird is sitting. The brooding birds do occasionally leave the nest to eat, drink, or bathe; that's when you can take a look.

If baby birds should hatch, they have to be given proper rearing food. Unfortunately we have practically no experience to go on with mynahs. But considering what other members of the starling family feed their young, we may assume that the following items are appropriate: ant pupae, mealworm larvae, hard-boiled egg, and food for softbills. Add to this, if possible, grasshoppers, caterpillars, grubs, flies, and other insects.

Obtaining insects in needed quantities presents a problem. Perhaps baby mynahs could be given some of my standard mynah concoction (see page 40), but I don't know how it would agree with them. The whole question of nutrition for mynah nestlings is still virgin territory.

I would expect that baby mynahs stay in the nest for about 20 days. Then they are fed a few days longer by their parents until they learn to take care of themselves. Probably the birds could raise two broods per year.

Keeping a pair of mynahs or several mynahs practically always diminishes their interest in imitating the human voice. Under these circumstances the birds are too busy with their own lives.

## If You Start Out with a Nestling

Should you be lucky enough to get a mynah still at the nestling stage, i.e., a bird that

In order to get at their favorite food—fruits growing on trees—more easily, mynahs have acquired impressive climbing skills.

# Raising Mynahs

has not yet learned to fly, conditions are ideal for the bird to become very tame and learn to talk. But you also have to take some extra precautions with such a "baby" that would be unnecessary with an older mynah.

## Housing the Nestling

First of all, a nestling needs different accommodations than a grown bird. He needs an imitation parental nest. This can easily be constructed out of a small cardboard box or a flowerpot of appropriate size. Fill whatever you have chosen as a container with dry, clean hay or straw and make a hollow in the middle that is about the size of the mynah. Then put the bird in this artificial nest, where he will remain for the time being.

## How to Feed the Nestling

A nestling mynah has not yet learned how to go after food himself. He simply opens his bill in a wide gape and waits for you—his surrogate parent—to feed him. This behavior is typical of nestlings of nidicolous species, i.e. birds that are reared for a time in a nest, and it plays an important role in the family life of these birds. By opening his bill wide, the nestling displays bright, usually yellow or reddish "color

Above: A pair of mynahs during a courtship display in the air. The picture was taken by Konrad Wothe in southern India. Below: Common Mynah (*Acridotheres tristis*) sitting in the entry of its nest cavity.

signals" inside the gape. Many nidicolous baby birds also have a light-colored flange around the edge of the mandibles that serves as an optical signal as well. The colors of the flange and inside the mouth are meant to convey one thing, namely: This is where the food goes, please! These colorful signals act as an important stimulus for feeding behavior in the parent birds, and they are made even more urgent by the nestlings' begging calls. A baby bird that is very hungry begs as loudly as it can and opens its bill in a wide gape. When it has had enough to eat, it sits quietly with shut beak. This way the hungriest nestling has the best chance to get fed first when a parent arrives with a mouthful of food. And for you as foster parent, it is useful to know that your mynah nestling will beg and display his gape when he's hungry and will be quiet and content when he's had enough to eat. However, if he stays quiet too long, for several hours perhaps, this is a sign than he is ill or that it is too cold for him.

What should you feed a mynah that still depends on outside help to eat, and how do you get the food into his gullet? You can start with the concoction I described on page 40. If you supplement this with insects like grasshoppers, crickets, and freshly hatched (white) mealworms, as well as some raw, fresh fruit, such as grapes, plums, and bits of peeled orange, you will provide the young mynah with a healthy diet. But feed only small morsels, never big pieces, no matter how huge the bird's gullet may seem. Also follow the rule that it is better to give several small portions

# *Raising Mynahs*

a day—preferably every hour or so—than one or two big ones.

It is not all that simple to get small bits of food into a bird's beak by hand. Our fingers are too clumsy for this task. Half the food misses and piles up all around the bill rather than disappearing in it. The best tool for this job is tweezers. But the tweezers have to be flexible so that you can hold the food without having to squeeze with all your might, and the ends must be blunt. Never use pointed tweezers. A wrong move of your hand or the bird's head while the tweezers are inside the gape could cause serious injury.

Let's assume that you have a bit of food between the ends of the right kind of tweezers and the bird is begging, reaching his head with the wide open gape toward your hand expectantly. All you have to do now is to guide the tweezers carefully above the bill and drop the food into it. The bird can swallow without any further help because the tongue moves freely and propels the food downward. There is consequently no need for you to reach into the bird's mouth or even further with the tweezers.

If the young mynah does not like what you've given him, he'll try to get rid of it by tossing his head back and forth. There may be any reason for rejecting a morsel: The bird may be full; the morsel may be too large, too cold, or too hard; or the taste may be unfamiliar. Animals are just as conservative in their food habits as most humans.

In most cases, however, a bird will swallow something new if it is tasty. Never

force your mynah to eat something he obviously doesn't want. You *can* use force; all you have to do is stick the food down far enough, and the bird won't be able to spit it out again. But before you resort to this method, ask yourself whether the bird may not simply have had enough to eat, or whether the food might be too cold because it came straight from the refrigerator, or whether it is a week old and has gone sour.

It is best to use tweezers with rounded ends when feeding a nestling that is still begging for food. Give it small amounts several times during the day.

In spite of this rather lengthy discussion, hand-feeding is rarely problematic with birds the size of mynahs that eat fruit as well as animal proteins. But, as everyone knows, food not only enters the body but also leaves it in the form of indigestible remains and waste products. In the case of the young of nidicolous birds, nature has solved the problem of keeping the nest

# *Raising Mynahs*

clean very cleverly: The mushy droppings are contained in an elastic membrane like garbage in a plastic bag. This "sac" is usually produced right after food intake. The parent bird waits for it to appear, then picks it up with his bill and carries it off some distance from the nest, where he drops it.

A nestling usually turns around a bit in the nest before depositing his droppings, raises his rump to the level of the nest's edge, and then produces the droppings. You can pick them up easily with your tweezers and get rid of them. As long as the droppings are soft but still contained in the sac, this is a good sign that the food is agreeing with the bird and the digestion is working properly. Any change in diet will initially result in runnier droppings, but this is no cause for alarm yet. Only if the droppings are bubbly and very runny is it time to review the diet.

A young mynah will still display his gape and expect to be fed even after he has left the nest and has learned to fly (see page 50). This is normal because in nature the fledglings are still fed for a while by the parents. Gradually they learn to supplement the feedings by finding their own food. When your mynah reaches this stage, make sure there is always a small amount of ready-to-eat food in the cage so that he practices becoming independent.

While his first feathers grow in, a young mynah needs a lot of energy, and his only source of energy is the food he eats. It is therefore important that you feed him plenty. If you skimp now, the bird will later develop so-called "bare zones" on the flight feathers of the wings and tail, which then have a striped appearance. Bare zones are formed by the absence of vanes in spots along the individual feathers, and they are a sign that there were not enough nutrients when the feathers were formed.

## The Importance of Warmth

Should your young mynah be only sparsely feathered (this is unlikely because most mynahs are at least a few weeks old when sold), he will need extra warmth. A 40-watt bulb about 12 inches above the nest (or even better, an infrared heat lamp) will make up for the warmth normally provided by the sitting parent birds. But be very careful not to overheat! The temperature should never be above 95° F (35° C), nor should it drop below 86° F (30° C). The bird will indicate when he is too hot by stretching head and neck as far as possible over the edge of the nest and panting with open bill, but he has no way of signaling that he is too cold. You can check, however, by taking the bird in your hand. If he feels cool, i.e., cooler than your hand, and if he hardly moves and no longer opens his beak to beg for food, this is a sure sign that the bird is hypothermic. In a warm room it is often enough to cover the bird with a woolen cloth, especially if his body is already covered with feathers.

## How the Feathers Develop

Feathers first develop inside their shafts, which push their way through the skin in the form of pinfeathers. The shaft forms a bluish white covering over the developing feather and is supplied at the base with blood that sustains the growth of the feather. The tip of the feather develops first and pushes through the sheath, which then dries out and becomes flaky. In the course of preening, the bird pulls each feather through his bill and nibbles off the brittle sheath, thus exposing the finished part of the new feather. The feather keeps growing from the shaft until it has reached its full length.

You have to watch out for the feather shafts if you are going to clip your bird's wings (see page 29). New feathers grow in after each molt, and if you cut the shaft of a developing feather it will bleed, sometimes quite heavily. You should avoid this if at all possible. So make it a rule never to cut feather shafts that are still supplied with blood; trim only fully grown feathers!

## When Your Mynah Leaves the Nest

After a few days your young mynah will be ready to leave the nest you have provided for him. He indicates his intention shortly before his first venture out by climbing on the edge of the box or flower pot instead of lying in the nest hollow when he begs for food. Now you have to see to it that the bird and the nest—to which he will return at first whenever he is tired—are located where a first excursion, whether on foot or through the air, will not end in a painful crash. The inexperienced mynah is not yet able to break his fall and may be in poor shape if he tumbles from a table to the floor, for instance.

In nature young mynahs don't leave the nest until they can fly at least a short distance. This is particularly true for species that nest high above the ground.

But birds that have been hand raised sometimes want to leave the nest before the flight feathers are quite ready to carry them. This may happen when they are very hungry and try to meet their caretaker halfway. In their eagerness they may lose their balance or fly awkwardly into a wall. The youngsters master basic flying at a certain point, but then they still have to learn more complex maneuvers, such as landing, which requires various braking techniques.

You can assist your mynah's first ventures by providing some perches for him to land on. Another aid is to let him hop onto your hand or, preferably, your index finger when he hops up on the edge of the nest. Then move your hand slowly back and forth and up and down. This forces the bird to actively maintain his balance. He will clutch your finger tightly in order not to fall. Then move your hand with the bird on it close to a branch with natural bark. If he doesn't hop or fly to this perch by himself after a while, induce him to hop over by withdrawing your finger after having placed it up against the branch. Make him change over from one hand to the other in a similar manner. This teaches the bird to hop from one perch to another, to approach a perch in the air from a short distance, and to cling to a hold. You will be amazed how quickly the young bird assimilates these new skills. After just a few days he will fly around and land as though he'd been doing it for years.

## Independent Eating

As your mynah learns to fly, he also begins to look for food himself, although he will still beg for a few days after leaving the nest. At this point you can put small morsels of food in his cage, and he will soon try to eat some of them on his own. However, at this age he can't yet manage completely without assistance from you. This transitional phase lasts about one week. Then he should be able to feed himself without any help. Of course you can spoil him and prolong his dependency if you keep responding to his begging calls and gestures and go on feeding him. But there is no harm—within reasonable limits, of course—in letting some hunger pangs prod the bird on to fend for himself.

## Dangers for the Fledgling Bird

When your young mynah no longer wants to return to his nest, you can transfer him to a cage. At this point he is not yet ready to be moved into an outdoor aviary. He first has to perfect his flying skills and be able to find and deal with food without any help at all.

A bird that has just learned to fly approaches dangerous situations as well as potentially harmful creatures with a trust that can easily lead to disaster. Being raised by humans, he has not been taught what to fear. Parent birds know dangers from their own experience and warn their young or fly off when an enemy appears. The young quickly grasp the connection between the warning call and the enemy, and when the parents take off in flight, they follow instantly. Remember that a hand-raised mynah is an easy target for dogs, cats, or other predators, and take appropriate precautions. It is also useful to know that a young mynah with only rudimentary flying skills can fly up from the ground or a low perch more easily than down from high places. So if your bird should escape during his first days with you and take refuge on your roof or a tall tree, you may have to wait a long time before he comes down again.

# How Mynahs Learn to Talk

I am assuming that you have a mynah or plan to buy one because you've heard stories about these birds' amazing gift for mimicking human speech as well as all sorts of other sounds. It is true that mynahs, like some other birds, learn to copy words and phrases so perfectly that it is impossible to tell who is talking, human or bird.

## Mynahs—Kings Among Mimics

Parrots and various parakeets reproduce the human voice, but in almost all cases the voice has a slight screeching undertone, and the words come out somewhat slurred, giving them a "parrot-like" quality. This is not true of a mynah's speech. It has happened repeatedly at our house that visitors have gone to look for me in the garden, which is next to our mynah aviary, because they heard human voices there and assumed I was there. And any robber would probably have made a quick getaway if he had heard—but not seen—Peter, my pet mynah, enunciate clearly in the exact tones of my voice, "You thief!"

We really don't know why mynahs and parrots are such good mimics. With some bird families the talent for imitation seems to be in the blood. This is true of the starlings. Even our ordinary field starlings are masters at this skill. Their own innate song sounds primitive to our ears, because it consists of a series of harsh, rasping sounds. But they amplify their utterances by including sounds and voices they hear around them. Thus, if you listen attentively you can detect in a starling's song the

croaking of frogs, the quacking of ducks, the squeak of a barn door, and the calls of other birds. These are sounds and voices normally encountered by birds in nature. The human voice is absent because wild birds keep their distance from people.

We know that in some species the young learn their songs from the male parent because they hear the characteristic sequence of tones over and over as nestlings and later on as fledglings. A young bullfinch, for instance, learns the song of his species from his male parent, but if he is raised in captivity and people whistle to him, he will imitate all kinds of tunes. There are bullfinches that learn entire songs this way.

In the mimicry of mynahs and many species closely related to them, such as the starlings, two factors may be working together: the learning that takes place during the first few weeks of life and a general, lifelong facility for reproducing sounds.

## You Cannot "Loosen" a Bird's Tongue

The erroneous assumption that a bird's tongue has to be "loosened" before he can talk used to be quite common and is still encountered occasionally today. This is, of course, pure nonsense. A mynah's tongue is attached to the lower mandible by only a bit of skin; the front of the tongue tapers to a thin tip, and in the back there are two lateral extensions, which serve to propel the food down into the gullet. (A parrot's tongue, by contrast, is thicker and more solid because of these birds' different

# How Mynahs Learn to Talk

eating habits.) The only thing that could be "loosened" on a mynah's tongue is the connection to the lower mandible. But this would mean cutting the tongue out. After such an operation the bird would starve to death because it could no longer eat.

## A Story About a Mynah

I don't want to raise your expectations concerning mynahs too high, for experience has shown that not every one of these birds becomes an accomplished talker, and some imitate very little or not at all. However, I want to share at least one of the many stories told about the skills of these talking birds. The following story is taken from an article Heinz Geck published in 1952 in the monthly magazine *Die gefiederte Welt (Feathered World)*.

"My friend in Delhi had given me the use of his bungalow in the mountains for the time he would be away on leave in Europe. I saw him off on the boat that was to take him there, and the next day I drove to the mountains. But whom did I hear shouting inside the bungalow when I arrived? None other than my friend, who had presumably been sailing westward aboard the *Sibajak* for the past twenty-four hours at thirteen knots an hour. Luckily it was the middle of the day, or I might have begun to believe in ghosts, for Indian nights have a magic of their own. As it was, I figured somebody was pulling a trick on me and entered. But there was not a soul in the entire house, and now I did begin to wonder. At that moment my friend

said 'Shut up!' in Malay, and a house servant answered in a subdued but nasty voice, *'Saja toewan!'*

"I leapt back to the veranda, where I was greeted by loud, jeering laughter. There on the door frame sat a kind of crow that looked me over disparagingly with its crafty eyes.

"'Well, you ugly bird,' the creature addressed me with a sneering laugh.

"'Well, I never . . .' I started to say when the crow (which was, of course, a mynah) growled, 'Where is that Ali? He's the laziest, most good-for-nothing *djongos* on the face of the earth. *Makan die mana* (Where's the food), Ali?'

"A moment later Ali, who had been in the kitchen wing, entered with the *makan* (food).

"'Ali, you disgrace in the sight of Allah!' the mynah snarled.

"Ali glanced at the black bird with a mixture of exasperation and amusement and then turned to me. 'Don't believe everything he says, sir. This *tjuuhoeng* (the Malayan word for mynah) has a wicked soul.'

"'Hahahaha,' was the *tjuuhoeng*'s response.

"This bird had a large vocabulary and could speak and whistle in the exact tone of every person living in the house. He created no end of confusion with his calls to the servants. He whistled to the dogs, ordered coffee, called for shaving water and a bath—everything in perfect imitation of his master. Now I heard someone yawn unabashedly, jump out of bed, whistle a few notes, and gargle with abandon. I found it hard to believe, but it was only the mynah going through his morning routine. When I sat down to breakfast, he greeted me cordially and immediately answered for me. I tried to make friends with him, but that made him think I was a junk dealer and caused him to tell me off with startling vehemence in Pidgin English: 'Shut up now! I'm not buying anything. Nothing, you hear!'

"By afternoon the *tjuuhoeng* had my intonation down pat, and between noon and sundown he called for Ali forty-four times in my voice. When I finally called for the servant myself, Ali had long since decided to ignore the calls. . . .''

## Hints to Help You Find a Good Mimic

• Buy a Greater India Hill Mynah. The best talkers are found in this subspecies.
• Buy a young bird. At a young age birds accept humans quickly and learn best, even if they start out timid. Birds that were full-grown when captured hardly ever overcome their shyness of people and don't learn to talk at all or only very little.
• Buy your mynah in mid- to late summer. Since these birds mate between April and August, your chances for getting a youngster are best during this season.
• Stay away from a mynah that has changed owners several times. These birds either don't perform at all (which may be the reason why they are passed on) or repeated changes in environment have made them nervous and shy.

• Make sure the bird you're buying is healthy (see page 15).
But finally you have to take a chance and hope for the best.

## No Rules or Magic Formulas for Teaching Mynahs

Thanks to some connections I had, I acquired my first two mynahs at the end of May directly from an importer. The birds were, for all practical purposes, still nestlings and could not yet fly. They still had to be fed, and in the process they became hand tame.

Both were Greater India Hill Mynahs. One of them, Peter, I kept, and the other I gave away. Peter was not a remarkable talker. That probably had to do with the fact that I kept him in the house for only about a year and then moved him to an outdoor aviary, where he was happier but was no longer interested in learning to imitate.

Nevertheless, his first efforts were promising. As i tell you what and how Peter learned, you will see that there is no magic formula that produces results.

The first imitation Peter produced was the flutelike call of the orioles in our garden. They had arrived back from their winter quarters in Africa at about the time I acquired Peter. So he was exposed to the orioles' melodious tune all day long while he was still in the nest. After a few weeks he mastered it himself, and he remembered this short tune for many years until he

# How Mynahs Learn to Talk

suddenly gave up singing it. As long as it was part of his repertoire I only heard it in the summer—that is, when the orioles were around.

Next Peter learned to say his name. He had of course heard it often from the very beginning.

Now you might think, as I did, that mynahs learns to copy primarily what they hear a lot or what people keep repeating to them. But that is not the case.

One day, when Peter was already living in the aviary in the garden, a friend arrived with a dachshund by the name of Nicko. The dog barked and jumped around the aviary wildly. My friend noticed that I disapproved, and she shouted "Nicko! Nicko, come here!" at the top of her voice. She had to repeat her command five or six times before the dachshund obeyed. Meanwhile Peter had gotten quite upset, and the next day he shouted "Nicko! Nicko!" in a perfect imitation of my friend's voice. "Nicko" remained part of his vocabulary for a few months, and then he forgot it.

You might conclude that mynahs learn best when in a situation of stress. That is what I now thought. So when I wanted Peter to learn a few impressive swear words, I smashed a pile of plates on the floor with an earsplitting clatter, and then cursed. Peter was not in the least impressed and never learned to curse.

Then my daughter decided to teach him "Yes, Peter, honey," by repeating it over and over. He did learn to say this and never forgot it as long as he lived. Eventually he also permanently mastered the phrase "You thief!" which I taught him by the same drill method. But many other

things we said or whistled for his benefit he paid no attention to.

On the other hand, various sounds that we hardly noticed must have made an impression on the mynah because he started to copy them. One of them was the metallic "plink-plink-plink" from a nearby black-smith shop. Then there were my coughing fits when I had caught a bad cold one winter. Suddenly Peter was coughing like an old hand. He coughed for several years, but only in the winter; it made no difference whether anybody in the family had a cold at the time or not. Peter also learned to imitate my dog whistle and called by name the hunting dog I had had when Peter first arrived. When I got a different dog two years later that had a different name, Peter stuck with the name he knew and never learned the new one. As you can see, the conclusions contradict each other:

- A mynah learns what he hears often.
- A mynah learns what he hears once.
- A mynah learns what he hears in a frightening or upsetting context.
- A mynah refuses to learn anything at all in a stressful situation.
- A mynah retains what he has learned for life.
- A mynah forgets what he has learned.

This demonstrates that there are no hard and fast rules governing the learning process. This is true not only for mynahs but also for other mimicking birds, as any parrot owner will confirm. You can say or whistle something you want your parrot to say until you're blue in the face. No dice. Then one day the bird surprises you with a phrase or expression that was not meant for anybody else's ears.

# How Mynahs Learn to Talk

## What May Incline a Mynah to Talk

In one of his books, Konrad Lorenz, the famous expert on animal behavior, tells about a tame crow that learned to talk. The crow was not kept in a cage and flew around at large. One day it disappeared. When it turned up again a few days later, it could say: "They got 'im in a trap!" Clearly the crow had gotten caught in a snare set by some boys in the neighborhood—an extremely frightening as well as painful experience that taught the bird one of its first sentences.

Don't worry! You need not resort to traps to get your mynah to talk. Surely that is not a defensible method. In view of the experience I've had with mynahs, I would generalize that birds are *more* inclined to repeat (a) things that they hear a lot, and (b) things they can associate with specific situations. Let me give a few examples. When you enter the mynah's room in the morning, you greet him.

• This little scene is repeated every day. The anticipation of seeing you and the

Not every mynah takes to mimicking. Innate calls and "songs," too, are recited with gusto and often at a high pitch.

opening of the door are exciting to the bird, and he'll probably soon learn your morning greeting.

Or: The phone rings and you say "Hello."
• This happens several times a day. The ringing of the phone and your going to answer it are special events for the mynah, and he will probably soon learn your way of answering the phone.

Or: Someone is at the door. The dog barks. Perhaps you say to him "Be quiet!" or "Go away!"

This, too, is a routine sequence of events. The sound of the doorbell and your going to the door create a stir, and the mynah will probably soon imitate the bell, the barking, or your command to the dog.

There are many small scenes like this in everyday life, scenes that happen repeatedly the same way and that create some excitement in the bird that you do not even notice.

## The Mynah's Calls or "Songs"

Apart from the sounds a mynah learns to reproduce, he also has his own innate calls or "songs." I've already mentioned these. They are loud and usually high-pitched. You can be practically deafened in a small room because mynahs sing with great persistence, particularly in the morning and evening. If you think that this noise would drive you crazy, give up the idea of owning a mynah.

All I can wish you is that your mynah is or becomes a good mimic. Patience on your part, quiet relaxed dealing with the bird, his ease with you, and proper care and nourishment all contribute to success.

# *If Your Mynah Gets Sick*

You hardly ever see a sick bird in nature. Any bird that is not in top health—because of old age or some other reason—quickly becomes prey to one of its many enemies or hides somewhere to die. The only remains you may come across are a few feathers and bones, and there is no telling the cause of death at that point.

## Signs of Illness

The onset of an illness is usually apparent in a bird that lives in captivity, and since there are effective treatments. the patient can often be saved. But I warn you against trying your hand at doctoring unless you have the appropriate experience. It is easier to do harm than to help. Leave the job of finding the right cure to the veterinarian.

A sick bird sits still, with puffed-up feathers and closed eyes, and takes no notice of his surroundings. Often the area around the vent—the opening which serves for sexual purposes and for the discharge of urine and excreta—is dirty, and feces are extruded with great difficulty or not at all. The bird's usual cheerfulness has

If you find your mynah in his cage all puffed up like this, with eyes closed, and completely indifferent to his surroundings, he is sick.

vanished, and all singing, whistling, and mimicking has stopped. Symptoms of this kind suggest some disease of the internal organs.

## Internal Diseases

Most internal diseases affect the respiratory system and the digestive tract. The most common ones are colds, pneumonia, diarrhea, cramps, and liver disease.

### Disorders of the Respiratory System
The usual causes of respiratory problems are drafts and abrupt changes in temperature. Birds that have been kept indoors and are suddenly moved to an outdoor aviary during cool weather are likely candidates for colds. So are birds whose cages are in the path of drafts between a door and window. Red swollen eyelids, coughing, sneezing, and breathing through the open beak are symptoms of colds. The bird also has the apathetic look described above. The best treatment is to provide warmth (an even temperature of about 77° F (25° C), preferably through an infrared heat lamp. In a pinch a regular 40-watt light bulb will do. Add a dissolved antibiotic (Aureomycin or Terramycin) to the drinking water. Camomile tea is better than water, but whatever the mynah drinks should never be ice cold. If there is no improvement within two days, you should definitely call the vet.

### Disorders of the Gastrointestinal Tract
Problems of the digestive system are often

associated with colds, or they can be caused by an improper diet or spoiled food. The first step is remove all food remains promptly every day.

Diarrhea is the first sign of trouble. The droppings are not only runny but almost watery and often bubbly. The bird loses his usual gusto for eating or hardly eats at all and sits in his cage listlessly.

To provide relief you should supply warmth (as for colds), replace the drinking water with weak black tea, and feed the bird cooked rice with hard-boiled egg (in addition to his normal food).

If your sick mynah lives in an indoor cage, you can leave him there to recuperate. But if he is in an aviary, whether indoors or outdoors, it is better to catch him and place him in a smaller cage until he feels better. It is easier to check on him there and to shine a heat lamp on him.

### Intestinal Parasites

Another cause for stomach and intestinal problems is internal parasites that the bird may have picked up before you bought him or that he may get from eating insects. Birds with intestinal parasites lose weight in spite of eating ravenously and eventually lose their strength. If you take a stool sample to the veterinarian, he can analyse it for parasites and prescribe effective medication against them. In most cases it is now possible to get rid of intestinal parasites quite easily.

### Obesity

Disease and death is often brought on by obesity and resulting liver damage. Mynahs that are kept in small cages where they do not get enough exercise get too fat very easily.

I can't repeat often enough that prevention is better than any cure. Prevent weight gain by giving your mynah as much freedom of movement as possible and feeding him a proper diet. Small portions of chopped greens like lettuce, chickweed, parsley, or spinach mixed in with the regular food will go a long way in keeping your mynah healthy.

## Fractures and External Injuries

It is difficult for an untrained person to detect internal diseases in a mynah. External injuries, on the other hand, are clearly evident. You'll have no trouble telling when a bird has been hurt. A broken wing hangs down and cannot resume its normal position. If a leg is broken, the bird favors it by not stepping on it. Fractures are usually caused by collisions with hard surfaces (see page 30) or by other accidents. But since birds, like most animals, have a higher pain threshold than humans, broken bones and injuries to skin and muscle don't bother them too much. Problems arise only if a fracture doesn't heal properly or if the bones set wrong. Then the bird's locomotion may be severely impaired.

Because of these possible complications you should have a veterinarian take a look at any fracture unless you have experience splinting bones. It is important that you consult the veterinarian *immediately*, not after a few days. By that time the bones may have begun to grow together wrong, and it may be too late to reset them. Broken wings are especially tricky because the wing should be restored to full use again if at all possible. The veterinarian will decide whether to apply a splint or immobilize the wing—the way it is usually done with smaller birds—by tying it against the body in its normal rest position.

Fractures of the wings need the attention of a veterinarian. The injured wing should either be splinted or tied to the body in normal rest position.

Different kinds of leg fractures require different treatments. A broken femur cannot be splinted because that part of the leg is too closely attached to the body. In an open fracture the ends of the broken bones have to be carefully pushed back beneath the skin. Then the wound is disinfected and the bird kept as quiet as possible. Remove all perches from the cage, and place the bird in a warm, dark spot (with enough light, however, so that the bird can see to eat). Fractures of the leg or the tarsus are usually easy to splint. A plaster cast over absorbant cotton also works well.

Fractures take two to three weeks to heal. Broken toes don't need to be treated because they heal if left alone. But if a toe is not just broken but practically torn off, it is better to cut it off with scissors and apply some healing powder or cream and styptic cotton to the stump. The wound will soon heal.

Skin and flesh wounds are also treated with healing powder or salve. They usually mend very quickly and hardly bother the bird at all.

## Parasites of the Skin and Plumage

Birds living indoors are rarely plagued by ectoparasites, that is, parasites that inhabit their host's exterior rather than internal organs (the intestines, stomach, lungs, and liver) as endoparasites do. The main pests that bother birds are fleas, lice, and mites. They usually spread from bird to bird through direct contact. In an outdoor aviary they can be transmitted to mynahs by sparrows and other wild birds.

The *red bird mite* sucks its host's blood. These parasites stay hidden during the day in cracks and crannies and attack the sleeping birds at night. The best way to prevent an infestation is to disinfect the nest boxes, the cage, and the surrounding area thoroughly and frequently.

The *scaly-leg mite* establishes itself between the horny scales on the legs and toes. The scales then no longer form a smooth surface but stick up. A calcereous crust forms on the affected areas, which should be dabbed with Vaseline unless the veterinarian prescribes a different medication (Eurax Cream or the injectable medication Ivermectin [Equalan]).

# If Your Mynah Gets Sick

*Feather mites* attack the feathers, causing the plumage to look rough and moth-eaten. But there are now good antidotes for these pests, too.

If you dust or spray your mynah with a medication against parasites (tick and flea powder for dogs containing pyrethrin or cabaryl), make sure that none of it gets into the bird's eyes, nostrils, or bill. If he absorbs significant amounts of it, this may have serious consequences.

## The Molt

The feathers of a bird wear out with time. Extensive flying, brushing against twigs and branches, and other mechanical demands are hard on the feathers' tips in particular. Nature's wise solution to this problem is to provide an entirely new set of feathers periodically.

We speak of molt when a bird loses its old plumage and grows a new one. When the small feathers covering the body are replaced, the contour feathers are molting, and when the primaries and secondaries on the wings and the tail feathers are replaced, the flight feathers are molting. Many birds molt both types of feathers simultaneously. Mynahs molt between August and October.

Under normal circumstances, a molt never leaves a bird naked. At most there may be a few temporary bald spots on the head. Nor does a mynah lose enough flight feathers all at once to ground it. The primaries and secondaries come out one at a time, leaving so-called bare skin spots on the spread wings where the replacement feathers have not yet grown in. These bare skin spots always form a symmetrical pattern on the two wings. If a molt proceeds in normal fashion, you may not even be aware of it. Your only clue may be some feathers on the cage floor. Nor is the bird in any way incapacitated if he is in good health.

During the molt the plumage is replaced. New feathers grow in after the old ones are lost.

Still, you should keep an eye out for signs of molt. Growing new feathers makes higher demands on the metabolism, and the bird should receive an optimal diet at this time.

If your mynah doesn't molt properly or fails to molt at all within a year, there is something wrong with his diet. Perhaps you are feeding him too one-sidedly, depriving him of necessary vitamins, calcium, and salts. If you notice that the molt is coming to a halt or that the new feathers are not growing in properly, call the veterinarian at once. In most cases, doses of the right vitamins, exposure to an infrared lamp, and daily spraying with lukewarm water will take care of the problem.

The so-called "molt facilitators" that you can buy at pet stores are usually totally ineffective.

## First-Aid Kit for a Mynah

You should have a few standard medications and other items handy so that you don't have to make a trip to the veterinarian for every minor problem. Set up a small kit for your bird, but remember that medications lose their efficacy after a while and have to be replaced. You will want to have the following:

• A heat lamp (infrared lamp) of 40 or 60 watts.
• Antibiotics to combat infections (Aureomycin, Terramycin).
• Healing salve and powder for open wounds.
• Styptic cotton.
• Band-aids, gauze bandages.
• Scissors and pointed tweezers.
• A disinfectant for cleaning the cage.

One last point: Any time you need to treat your mynah, you'll have to catch and hold him, an experience that is in itself frightening and upsetting to the bird (see page 68). Therefore, try to perform whatever has to be done calmly, efficiently, and quickly. Think ahead and figure out exactly each step you need to take; otherwise you may forget something, and the bird will have to suffer through the trauma twice.

# Understanding Mynahs

## A Brief Introduction to Ornithology

To learn to understand mynahs, you first need some background information about birds in general. That is why I want to preface this chapter with a short introduction to ornithology.

The most obvious difference that sets birds apart from all other vertebrates is their plumage. The head and body are covered with small feathers, which cover up all irregularities of shape and give the bird its smooth, streamlined contours. The large feathers on wings and tail provide steerage and the necessary surface area for flying. The feathers are made up of a horny substance that is also found in the scales of reptiles, from which birds are descended. Birds still have some horny scales left, namely on their legs. And the bill, which consists of bone, is also covered with a horny layer.

Birds are warm-blooded, like mammals. Their body temperature is about 106° F (41° C). If the surrounding temperature is cold, the bird puffs up its feathers. This way a lot of air is trapped between the individual feathers and creates an insulating layer that keeps in the body warmth. When the bird gets too warm it flattens its feathers, pressing out the air between them. Birds cannot sweat. They lack sweat glands. If a bird is still too hot when the feathers are completely flattened, it opens its bill wide and pants like a dog, causing moisture to evaporate from the oral cavity. Or it may take a bath to cool down.

Most birds can fly. There are only a few flightless species, such as the ostrich or the penguin, whose wings have evolved into "fins" used to swim under water. The flight of birds is one of nature's works that is close to a technical miracle. Any attempt to explain how a bird flies would be too involved for a book of this length. The amazing thing is that birds don't have to learn to fly. At a certain point they simply know how. They may not fly with consummate skill at first, but they do well enough to survive, and they quickly master the minor subtleties required mostly for landing and takeoff. There are other adaptive mechanisms for a life spent mostly on the wing. Thus birds have so-called air sacs that extend from their lungs throughout the body. This system allows for much better utilization of the air that is breathed in. Air sacs between the powerful wing muscles also prevent overheating on long and arduous flights. The bones are very light but strong and partially hollow. Even the skull has a number of hollow spaces to keep the bird's "prow" light.

All birds lay eggs, and most species incubate them. Among the exceptions are the brood parasites—like the cuckoo—which lay their eggs in the nests of other species. Nestlings are either nidicolous (reared in the nest) or nidifugous (leaving the nest soon after hatching). Mynahs belong among the former. They are quite helpless when hatched and need parental care for days or weeks before they can fly and are ready to leave the nest. Nidifugous

A Java Hill Mynah (*Gracula religiosa religiosa*) in its natural setting.

# *Understanding Mynahs*

birds like chickens, ducks, and geese are able to move about and swim within hours of hatching. They usually eat their own food from the beginning and follow their parents around. They are born with a covering of warm down, which is gradually replaced with true feathers.

The richness of variety that characterizes the world of birds carries over to the foods they eat and the manner of consumption. But one rule applies to them all: No bird can go without food for long. Small birds can die of starvation if deprived of food for even a few hours, especially if it is cold. On the average a bird has to consume about a third of its body weight in food a day. Indigestible parts of what is eaten pass through the digestive tract and are eliminated through the cloaca. Sometimes a bird spits things out of the beak. These are usually unpalatable bits like hairs, feathers, and chitinous parts of insects that have formed small clumps in the bird's stomach and are regurgitated. Mynahs, too, spit out clumps like this, particularly after eating a lot of mealworms.

Birds orient themselves mostly with the help of their eyes, but their hearing is also well developed. Otherwise all the calling and singing that birds do would be pointless. The olfactory sense is only rudimentary in

Above left: Hill Mynah (*Gracula religiosa*). Above right: Yellow-faced or Papuan Mynah (*Mino dumontii*) from New Guinea, the Bismarck Archipelago, and the Solomons. Below left: Crested Mynah (*Acridotheres cristatellus*) from Central and South China, Indochina, and Taiwan; the bird was introduced into Luzon (Philippines) and Vancouver, Canada. Below right: Rothschild's Mynah (*Leucopsar rothschildi*).

birds, but the sense of taste is all the more keen. It is quite amazing how quickly a bird can decide, with the help of its tongue, whether a bit of food in its bill is tasty or not.

## How Long Have Mynahs Been Kept by Fanciers?

The Amsterdam Zoo had several mynahs as early as 1815, and the same zoo first displayed the Java Hill Mynah in 1852. The Greater India Hill Mynah was first exhibited in the London Zoo in 1859. Later, different races of mynahs were discovered, but none of them caught on with aviculturists, and they could often be correctly identified only by specialists. The Hill Mynahs with their lively nature and their talent for imitation were already established as popular pet birds.

## Mynahs Living in the Wild

The Hill Mynahs differ very little in their way of life. So there is no need to discuss the three subspecies separately here.

The area of distribution of mynahs extends from Southeast Asia to southern China. Here the birds live in pairs or small flocks in parklike landscapes dotted with tall trees or groups of trees. Dead limbs sticking out of the tops of trees are their favorite haunts. Toward sunset they become especially lively and noisy, calling and answering back and forth until they finally retire to their sleeping places.

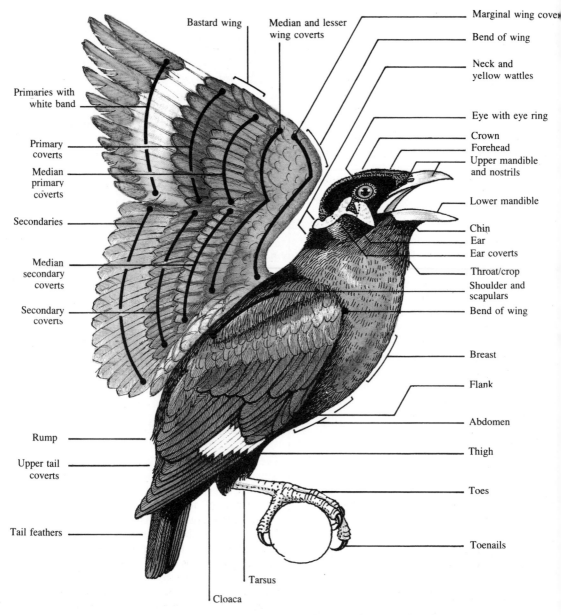

Bastard wing

Median and lesser
wing coverts

Marginal wing cover

Bend of wing

Neck and
yellow wattles

Primaries with
white band

Eye with eye ring

Crown

Forehead

Upper mandible
and nostrils

Primary
coverts

Median
primary
coverts

Lower mandible

Chin

Secondaries

Ear

Ear coverts

Throat/crop

Median
secondary
coverts

Shoulder and
scapulars

Bend of wing

Secondary
coverts

Breast

Flank

Abdomen

Rump

Thigh

Upper tail
coverts

Toes

Tail feathers

Toenails

Tarsus

Cloaca

Anatomy of a mynah: What is where on your bird?
Having a clear idea of bird anatomy is particularly
useful when you talk with your veterinarian.

# *Understanding Mynahs*

## Calls and Other Sounds

The calls or songs of mynahs are, for the most part, far from melodious or pleasant to our ears. On the contrary—as you will realize as soon as you bring home one of these birds—they include shrill whistling, gurgling, and screeching noises that may be innocuous enough under open skies but that can get on your nerves and be a positive nuisance when reverberating inside a room.

Mynahs are excellent and powerful flyers. When in the air they stretch the head far forward, and the beating of the wings can be heard from afar.

## Nutrition

In the wild, mynahs live primarily on wild figs and other fruit. But they also eat insects and small vertebrates, such as small lizards, which they crush and kill with their strong beaks and then swallow whole.

## Catching the Young Birds

The mating period of mynahs is from April until August. This means that from May to July you have the best chance of obtaining a truly young bird from a dealer. Most mynahs that are for sale were taken from their nests by natives and hand-raised. Thus, they are tame. Birds that were caught when mature often remain shy and suspicious for the rest of their lives. Needless to say, they are not likely to become good talkers.

To make it easier to get at the nestlings and to avoid having to split open trees or tree limbs to reach the nest, artificial nesting cavities are set up for mynahs in one district in Assam (India). These bottle-shaped, artificial nests are made of bamboo and straw, measure about six feet in length, and have an entry hole near the bulging middle section. The baby mynahs are sold by the natives and then taken mainly to Calcutta, from where they are shipped to fanciers all over the world.

## The Nest of a Mynah

Mynahs prefer tree holes about 30 to 60 feet above ground. The bottom of the hole is thickly padded with grass, leaves, and feathers. Ordinarily a clutch consists of only two to three eggs colored a lovely bluish green with brown dots or patches. The young are nidicolous and are fed by the parents for about two weeks before they learn how to fly and are ready to leave the nest.

# Are Mynahs Different from Other Birds?

Are mynahs fundamentally different from other birds? Not at all, in spite of their ability to learn to talk, whistle, cough, or whatever. They are exceptionally good mimics, but they are by no means the only birds to possess this skill. Still, mynahs are the unsurpassed masters.

In every other aspect of behavior mynahs are just like any other birds. And just like any other birds they perceive humans first and foremost as large, dangerous enemies from whom it is best to keep a safe distance. The reason this description does not seem to fit most mynahs one finds in a pet store is twofold: Most of these birds were taken from their nests when very young and were raised by people; and, secondly, mynahs are extremely gregarious creatures. As a result of these two facts, the birds eventually treat their caretakers like fellow birds and form strong attachments to them. *You* know that your mynah is a bird, but he doesn't know that you are a human. To him you are a member of his species.

## Humans As Bird Partners

A pair of birds belonging to a gregarious species often engages in what is called mutual preening. This means that one bird uses his bill to gently scratch places, such as the head and neck, that the partner cannot reach easily with his own bill.

No bird takes kindly to rude petting that messes up its plumage, possibly making the feathers stand up on end.

A tame bird sometimes lets his human friend stroke him gently with a fingernail. This feels good to him. What he does not like is if you dig in with all five fingers, perhaps even against the lie of the feathers. A cat or dog or other furred animal may put up with it, but not a bird. Feathers are extremely delicate and complex structures that break, split, or get tangled if roughly handled. Keeping his plumage in top shape is crucial to a bird's survival, and he therefore gets very vexed if his feathers are mussed. He'll have to spend hours smoothing them afterward and getting them back in some semblance of order.

One more reminder: In nature, being captured or caught hold of means certain death for a bird. So avoid taking hold of your mynah with your hands, even if he is tame, unless it is absolutely necessary, as in a case of injury where treatment is essential (see page 68).

A pair of birds that want to preen each other sit close together, both heads pointing in the same direction, practically arm in arm. If you have a mynah that has adopted you as his friend, there is one problem: He is small and you are enormous by comparison. Your head and hands have special meaning for him. He knows that your head is a head primarily because of the eyes. Your hands give him food and water and pet him, but they also inspire fear (at some point in his past human hands must have reached for him and grabbed him). Therefore he will try not to get too close to your hands but at the same time he wants a place where he can sit with his head next to yours. This place is usually

# *Understanding Mynahs*

your shoulder. Almost all tame birds choose their human partner's shoulder as their favorite perch. There they can get a good hold with their feet. The human head, especially if covered with straight, smooth hair, does not offer a very secure footing. So if your mynah displays his fondness for you by landing on your shoulder, take it as a compliment and don't shake him off. It is true that you might end up with some droppings on your dress or shirt, but there are ways of minimizing this risk. Make yourself a "shoulder bib."

But the mynah is not content to just sit on your shoulder. He also wants to preen you. He will use the tip of his bill to gently nibble at your hair, along the hairline, and at the ears. But don't let him get too close to your eyes. A hasty movement on your part or a misunderstanding on his might lead to an injured eye. It may also happen

A mynah will choose his human partner's shoulder to establish eye contact. A good way to protect your clothing against droppings is to wear a "shoulder bib" or simply drape a piece of cloth over your shoulder.

that the bird gets a little rougher and gives your ear a painful pinch with his sturdy bill. Don't respond by chasing him away angrily or shoving him off your hand. Instead, turn your head away, shield it with your hand, and scold him if you like. But keep in mind that the bird's intentions were of the best. Actually, you should be pleased at this sign that the bird has lost all shyness of you.

I have already mentioned that birds find their way around primarily by sight. They know exactly what their surroundings look like and register any change with distrust because in nature anything unfamiliar may hide an enemy. That is why most birds, and mynahs in particular, respond with panic when confronted with something unknown. My mynah Peter, who was ordinarily perfectly relaxed, would go into a frenzy every time someone wearing brightly colored clothing entered his room. He did this even if he knew the person. If you notice that something is upsetting your mynah and causing him to thrash around wildly in his cage, remove this something as quickly as you can. Not only could the bird hurt himself in his state of panic, but his terror might even bring on a heart attack.

Some mynahs are said to prefer women to men and vice versa. I have never observed any such predilection on the part of my birds (I have seen it in parrots, though, where it is quite common), but it can occur. If a bird favors a human female, this does not necessarily imply that the bird itself is a male. A more likely explanation is that the bird was raised by a woman.

# *Understanding Mynahs*

## Some Typical Patterns of Behavior

### Yawning
Mynahs yawn by suddenly opening their beaks wide for a second or two. They yawn mostly just before or after a nap.

### Stretching
Stretching is part of a bird's so-called comfort behavior. Mynahs stretch their wings either both at once and bent at an upward angle or one at a time out to the side, usually together with the leg of the same side. At the same time the head and neck are extended far forward.

### Scratching
Scratching is another example of comfort behavior. A mynah scratches its head and neck by raising a leg between body and wing.

### Sneezing
Mynahs sneeze occasionally. This is not necessarily a sign of a cold but often serves simply to clear the nasal passages. If a bird sneezes continually, however, and coughs in addition, it is sick (see page 57).

### Preening
Mynahs groom or preen themselves not only after bathing. Preening forms an integral part of any bird's elaborate daily ritual. All parts of the body, as far as they can be reached with the beak, are minutely examined for any irregularities in the plumage. Ordinarily this activity follows a routine, innate sequence. The large flight feathers of the wings and tail are restored to perfect smoothness by being pulled through the bill one by one. In the course of preening, the bird picks up some oil from the oil or uropygial gland, located just above the base of the tail, and distributes it over the entire plumage. This keeps the feathers elastic and water-repellant.

### Resting and Sleeping
When mynahs want to rest or sleep, they do not tuck their bills into their back feathers the way many other birds do but instead face straight ahead and hunker the head down between the shoulders. The eyes are closed. Mynahs often take short naps during the day.

### Drinking
Like most other birds, mynahs cannot suck up water when they drink. Instead they dip their bill in the water, pick up water with it, then raise the head and let the water run down into the gullet. Because of this drinking method, it is important that the drinking dish have a certain minimum depth or else the bird cannot fill its bill.

Unlike many other birds, mynahs sleep with their head pulled in between their shoulders. The eyes are closed. Please let your bird have a peaceful nap when he assumes this posture.

# Index

# Index